WITHDRAWN

MANUFACTURING DEVELOPMENT APPLICATIONS
GUIDELINES FOR ATTAINING QUALITY AND PRODUCTIVITY

**The Business One Irwin/
Institute of Industrial Engineers
Series in Engineering Management**

MANUFACTURING DEVELOPMENT APPLICATIONS
GUIDELINES FOR ATTAINING QUALITY AND PRODUCTIVITY

Andre McHose

The Business One Irwin/
Institute of Industrial Engineers
Series in Engineering Management

BUSINESS ONE IRWIN
HOMEWOOD, ILLINOIS 60430

We recognize that certain terms in this book are trademarks, and we have made every effort to print these throughout the text with the capitalization and punctuation used by the holder of the trademark.

This book presents characteristic experiences of people in industry. The narrative accounts are presented with fictional names, companies, products, and locations. Any resemblance to persons living or dead is purely coincidental.

© RICHARD D. IRWIN, INC., 1992

All rights reserved. No part of this publication may be reproduced, stored in a retrieval system, or transmitted, in any form or by any means, electronic, mechanical, photocopying, recording, or otherwise, without the prior written permission of the publisher.

This publication is designed to provide accurate and authoritative information in regard to the subject matter covered. It is sold with the understanding that neither the author nor the publisher is engaged in rendering legal, accounting, or other professional service. If legal advice or other expert assistance is required, the services of a competent professional person should be sought.

From a Declaration of Principles jointly adopted by a Committee of the American Bar Association and a Committee of Publishers.

Sponsoring editor: Jean Marie Geracie
Project editor: Ethel Shiell
Production manager: Ann Cassady
Jacket designer: Image House, Inc.
Art coordinator: Mark Malloy
Compositor: TCSystems, Inc.
Typeface: 11/14 Palatino
Printer: R. R. Donnelley & Sons Company

Library of Congress Cataloging-in-Publication Data

McHose, Andre.
  Manufacturing development applications : guidelines for attaining quality and productivity / Andre McHose.
      p.   cm.
  Includes bibliographical references and index.
  ISBN 1-55623-572-0
  1. Quality control. 2. Labor productivity. I. Title.
TS156.M3878   1992
658.5′62—dc20   92–1078

Printed in the United States of America
1 2 3 4 5 6 7 8 9 0 DOC 9 8 7 6 5 4 3 2

PREFACE

In this book, I have attempted to provide a narrative account of people at work, detailing some of the things that take place inside the plant, on the production line, and in management offices. In contrast to the events that take place in the corporate offices as reported in weekly business journals, this book presents the drama that takes place in manufacturing plants as managers, engineers, and operators undertake their work in manufacturing.

I present sufficient detail for the reader to understand and learn about the technical aspects of the subject matter under discussion, along with the human scenario in the industrial theater. Each narrative chapter deals with a leading manufacturing subject, how problems in this area were solved, and how the development took place.

The scope of the material covers development applications in manufacturing engineering and management systems. All of the programs presented had a direct bearing on the productivity, product quality, and manufacturing cost. Hopefully the reader will enjoy the material, see some familiar situation, and gain some ideas that may be useful in his or her regular work.

I have prepared this book with the practicing industrial and manufacturing engineer in mind. The hands-on engineer, charged with the responsibility of finding solutions to the types of problems presented, will be able to relate the principles and tools illustrated to the needs in his or her manufacturing center.

For manufacturing managers—persons actively working on improving operating strategies—guidelines are presented in the development programs. Consultants in the service sector, interested in learning about problem solving in manufacturing, should find the material applicable to their work. For students, the material reveals how and why certain approaches are chosen for use from among the many principles and theories available.

The author wishes to acknowledge the contribution of those who have helped in the development of this book. For starters, I view this as an opportunity to "give something back." On the larger scale, there is a compelling need to improve industrial productivity and product quality.

Early in the preparation of several chapters, two of my sons, Michael and Robert McHose, reviewed the material and made several helpful suggestions. Carolyn Lawrence also read the early chapters. Her editing skills and suggestions contributed much to establishing the style and format of the material. Thomas Nash, publisher, *The Ridgefield Press*, was helpful in providing background on publishing matters.

As the material progressed, discussion sessions with John Campbell, Vice President for Manufacturing, Medical Laboratories Automation; Kenneth McVicar, (retired) Vice President and General Manager, MITRE Corporation; and Donald Studley, CPA, Donald Studley, PC were very helpful. The following people also reviewed the material and encouraged the project: Arnold Coldiron, Consultant, former Senior Vice President for Operations, the Carlon Company; and Dr. Earl Strong, Professor Emeritus of Management, The Pennsylvania State University. I should like to express my appreciation for their encouragement.

Any person who undertakes the commitment of writing a book has to focus on the project. Some routine things don't get done. I wish to express my appreciation to my wife, Joy, who has understood and supported this writer's commitment.

Finally, a book sees the light of day only through the recognition and work of a publisher. For the valuable and helpful suggestions on the material, I wish to thank Jeffrey Krames, Executive Editor; Jean Geracie, Manufacturing Acquisition Editor; Ethel Shiell, Project Editor; and the supporting staff of Business One Irwin. In addition I should like to gratefully acknowledge the helpful suggestions of Maura Reeves, Senior Editor; and Carey Gifford, General Manager, of The Industrial Engineering and Management Press, copublisher of this book.

Andre McHose

CONTENTS

CHAPTER 1	INTRODUCTION	1

Industrial Challenges, Productivity, and Quality, 1
Technical Aspects, Manufacturing Engineering and Systems, 2
Problems from Misapplication, Understanding Context, 5
Need for Continuous Development, Use of Services, 6
Format of Material, Chapter Subjects, 7
System Analysis, Design, and Synthesis, 8
Manufacturing Productivity and Economic Vitality, 9
Manufacturing Engineering, 9
Chapter Summary, 10

CHAPTER 2	PRODUCTIVITY	11

Importance of Productivity, Productivity Centers, 11
Productivity, Definition, Rates, 11
Factors Affecting Productivity, 12
   Narrative: HiTech Machine Company, 13
      Background, 14
      Improving Productivity, 15
      Establishing a Manufacturing Engineering Function, 21
      Upgrading Operating Systems, 21
      Improve Work Flow, 22
      Install More Productive Machine Tools, 23
      Support Quality Control Program, 24
      Set up Training Program, 24
   Investing in Manufacturing Engineering, 26
Chapter Summary, 35

CHAPTER 3	QUALITY	37

Machine Capability Study, Basis and Value of Quality, 37
   Narrative: CleanPack Company, 38

Process out of Control, 38
Background, 38
Company Startup, 39
The Machine, 39
Statistical Control, 41
Machine Capability Study, 42
Variables and Attributes, 44
Calculation of Average and Standard Deviation, 50
   Calculation of Range of Values (± 3 s), 51
   Study of Machine 2, 51
   Analysis of Capability Study, 53
Chapter Summary, 57

CHAPTER 4   **MATERIAL CONTROL SYSTEMS**   59

Narrative: The Quick-Power Company, 60
   Background, 60
   Problem, 60
   Management Review, 60
   Program, 60
   Development Program, 61
   Product Definition, 62
   Order-Processing System, 66
   Machine Scheduling, 68
   Part-Numbering Problem, 69
   Organization, 71
   Sales Forecast, 72
   Capacity Planning, 72
   Status Report, 73
   Manufacturing Assembly Chart, 76
   Indented Bill of Materials, 76
Material Control in Transition, 80
 Just in Time, 81
 Manufacturing Cells and Total Quality Control, 81
 Flexible Manufacturing Systems, 81
 MRP and Capacity-Driven Systems, 81
Chapter Summary, 82

Contents **xi**

CHAPTER 5	FACILITIES AND LAYOUT	84

       Narrative: Southern/Bell Furniture Company, 85
   Kinds of Layouts, 87
       Plant Consolidation/Integration at River Road, 91
       General Approach in Layout, 97
   Chapter Summary, 106

CHAPTER 6	COST REDUCTION	109

   Value Engineering, 109
       Narrative: Ted Kiel's Comsys Company, 110
   Organization and Responsibility, 112
   Cost and Standard Data, 113
   Planning Levels, 113
   Personnel Qualifications, 114
   Project Selection, 114
   Project Execution, 115
   Chapter Summary, 122

CHAPTER 7	TECHNICAL ANALYSIS	123

       Narrative: Home Novelty Products Company, 125
   Chapter Summary, 133

CHAPTER 8	ADVANCE MANUFACTURING PLANNING	135

   General Concepts, 136
       Preliminary Considerations, 136
       Prove-Out Concept, 137
       Automation Inputs, 137
       Personnel Aspects, 138
   An Automation Synthesis, 138
       Application of the Rationale, 140
       Steps in the Process, 140
       System Reliability, 145
   Hardware Sewing Automation, 149
   Chapter Summary, 150

CHAPTER 9	MANAGEMENT, TOOLS AND TECHNOLOGY	152

   Changes in Manufacturing Technology, 152
   Management Charts, 154

Useful Concepts and Graphical Tools, 160
    Product Life Cycles, 160
    Learning Curve, 160
    Travel Chart, 160
    Matrix, 161
    Economic Analysis, 161
    Computer Programs and Simulations, 161
    Malcolm Baldrige National Quality Award, 163
Concerns of Management, 164
Chapter Summary, 164

APPENDIX A	Operational Audit	167
APPENDIX B	Quality Control Chart	177
APPENDIX C	Engineering Economic Analysis	181
NOTES		184
GLOSSARY		189
BIBLIOGRAPHY		193
INDEX		199

LIST OF FIGURES AND TABLES

Figure 2–1	Development Program	20
Figure 2–2	Planar-Grid Assembly and Fixture	28
Figure 3–1	Schematic Drawing of Automated Production System	40
Table 3–1	Partial Data Set, Product Length, Machine 1	45
Figure 3–2a	Pattern from Machine 1	46
Figure 3–2b	Pattern from Machine 1 with Envelope	46
Figure 3–3	Sample Distribution, Machine 1	48
Table 3–2	Partial Data Set, Product Length, Machine 2	51
Figure 3–4	Pattern from Machine 2	52
Figure 3–5	Sample Distribution, Machine 2	53
Figure 3–6	Potential Sources of Variation in the System	55
Table 3–3	Machine Development Tasks	56
Figure 4–1	Application Chart	62
Figure 4–2a	Product Structure Tree Chart	63
Figure 4–2b	Indented Bill of Materials	63
Figure 4–3	Simplified Chart of Existing Order-Processing System	67
Figure 4–4	Status Report: Parts/Assemblies	74
Figure 4–5	Form of the Manufacturing Assembly Chart	77
Figure 4–6	Indented Bill of Materials Showing Generation of Assembly	78
Figure 5–1	Site/Layout Features	90
Table 5–1	Operating Level, River Road Site	94
Table 5–2	Basic Savings from Development Program	95
Table 5–3	Cost and Economic Data, Building/Consolidation Program	96
Figure 5–2	General Layout Concept	100
Figure 5–3	Project Schedule	101
Figure 5–4	Illustration, Layout Detail	105
Figure 6–1	Data Sheet, Cost Reduction Program	117
Figure 6–2	Extrusion Design Concept	118
Figure 6–3	Calculation of Saving	120

Figure 6–4	General Cost-Reduction Applications	121
Figure 7–1	Illustration of Hinge	127
Figure 7–2	Physical Analysis of Hinge Formation	130
Figure 7–3	Properties of Aluminum Alloy Selected	132
Figure 7–4	Hinge Trouble-Shooting Chart	133
Figure 8–1	Operation Flowchart	141
Table 8–1	Cycle Time and Balancing Worksheet	143
Figure 8–2	Distribution of Unadjusted Machine Cycle Times	144
Figure 8–3	Schematic Diagram of Automated System	146
Table 8–2	Requirements, Manual/Automated System	148
Figure 9–1	Development Considerations for Management	153
Figure 9–2	Management Charts	155
Figure 9–3	Industrial/Manufacturing Engineering Charts	157
Figure 9–4	Quality Control Charts	159
Figure A–1	Closed-Loop Feedback System	168
Figure A–2	Transient Response of System	168
Figure A–3	Focus of Results-Oriented Audit	170
Figure A–4	Documentation, Plant Systems, and Procedures	172
Figure A–5	Baldrige Award Criteria Framework	175
Figure B–1	Control Chart for Variables	178
Figure C–1	Factors in Economic Analysis	182

CHAPTER 1

INTRODUCTION

INDUSTRIAL CHALLENGES, PRODUCTIVITY, AND QUALITY

There are promising challenges for American industry in the 1990s. Managers, engineers, and workers in some notable companies are engaged in bringing about innovative changes in the way business operates. Strategic changes in manufacturing operations are taking place. The subject matter of this book presents characteristic experiences of people in manufacturing who are working on the significant problem areas and the subsequent development programs that have taken place to improve manufacturing productivity and product quality.

The subject matter is presented in the form of narrative accounts of development programs in manufacturing engineering and management systems. The objective of each program was to advance the technology in some problem area in the plant. More generally, management, in authorizing work on the programs, was seeking an increase in productivity, an improvement in quality, and/or a reduction in manufacturing cost.

American plants possess an array of features in size and characteristics. Each of the 360,000 manufacturing plants are in various stages of development. About 100,000 may be considered job shops, with about 30 employees or fewer. The material in this book addresses a broad spectrum of plants, including those that are about to move into their first new building and are thinking about production planning. They, too, want to improve productivity and product quality.

New businesses are always in the process of starting up, and older businesses are trying to catch up. Thus, traditional manufacturing engineering (for those seeking basic planning) and the newer manufacturing technologies (for those seeking this information) are both presented.

One might ask, why not start with an *integrated manufacturing production system* and *total quality control?* But those are goals—continuous process objectives. A lot of basic manufacturing planning must first be accomplished, in addition to having the full support and resources from the corporate office to the factory floor.

It would be nice to start with a *flexible manufacturing system*—the super-machine system that consists of a computer control network, NC machine tools, a materials-handling system, cutting tools, and work-holding devices. But, because of cost and other factors it is estimated that only about 400 such systems exist in the whole world!

This book gives examples of characteristic needs and problem areas in manufacturing and shows how the development programs met the specific needs. While each solution is not viewed as the only approach in all specific details, each program did meet the objectives of upgrading operations. The term *program,* as used here, simply describes the content of each application as it developed.

TECHNICAL ASPECTS, MANUFACTURING ENGINEERING AND SYSTEMS

The applications presented here focus on the technical aspects of manufacturing engineering and manufacturing management systems. This is not to suggest a single-minded technology-cult solution to manufacturing problems! It is just that good technology is essential and that some of this technology is the major focus of this book.

Further, while the applications are centered in manufacturing, they are only part of the process—extending from research and product design to sales and back again for refinements in the cycle. All functions can and do contribute to the productivity of an organization. The focus of this book is on the manufacturing scene.

The subjects of personnel matters, management style, and worker involvement are recognized as very important components of developing effective operations. Success in developing a system is derived from the actions of people in the plant who are supported by informed and progressive top management. And in fact, the success of the newer, more integrated manager-engineer-worker relationships in the factory requires a more flexible, closely related, less departmentally structured, team approach, focused on product quality and productivity along with other strategic management objectives.

The position taken is that an improvement in product quality and productivity is a consequence of good management, good engineering, and manufacturing technology, along with effective systems in the workplace.

The perceptive engineer or manager is, among other things, a student of human behavior. He or she may have seen "poor" systems work fairly well, and "good" systems not work at all. In these situations people's attitudes and the plant morale make a difference. Technology alone will not do it. The manner in which development is approached has a significant effect on the results.

Each narrative chapter tells an industrial story about a principal topic. While the material is not presented in traditional textbook format, explanatory technical detail and illustrations are provided, both within the narrative description and as supplementary material explaining the subject matter under discussion. The approach here has been to provide easy-reading "how-to" accounts on the subject areas presented. The reader may wish to consult appropriate texts or handbooks for further details and background.

This book is about development and solving manufacturing problems. It is not suggested that practicing engineers or managers will come across identical situations in their work. What can be gained however, is a familiarity with characteristic situations, and *how* and *why* certain principles were used to solve problems from among the scores of methodologies, equations, formulas, and theories available in standard texts.

To provide substance to the narrative programs, some technical detail is presented. Stephen W. Hawking relates in his book, *A Brief History of Time,* a comment someone told him, "each equation I included in the book would halve the sales."[1] However, I urge the reader not to feel intimidated by the technical content of the material. Hopefully, the value and practical use of the modest technical detail will be apparent.

We are a country with industries ranging from traditional to high-tech, and as a people we take up the latest concepts and the litany of buzzwords that sweep over the land. Some of the industrial programs have a special emphasis while others have been expanded to incorporate some of the standard industrial and manufacturing engineering technology. The beneficial effect is to catch management's attention to, and gain support of, the development process. A few of the more common industrial concepts follow.

Illustrative Concepts

AI (Artificial Intelligence): Computer system programs that produce results we would normally associate with human intelligence. These expert systems contain a knowledge base, an inference engine, and a user interface. Applications are being developed in many areas of business and professional work.

JIT (Just in Time): A closely controlled material acquisition and processing system driven by customer demand. Collectively the system includes quick response, work cells, progressive assembly, unique organizational features, and other related concepts.

MRP (Materials Requirement Planning) and the more extensive MRP II: From a business plan/master production schedule, the system utilizes product assembly bills of material, process routing, inventory, and lead-time data to determine make-or-buy requirements and order release dates. In the process, capacity planning and feasibility are determined so as to meet or modify the production schedule.

There are other inventory systems such as the "vintage" ABC classification, which divides inventory into three classes to provide close control of high cost-parts; another inventory system, EOQ (Economic Order Quantity), seeks an order size that minimizes the net cost between ordering cost and carrying cost.

TQC (Total Quality Control): The support and participation of the entire organization and system in achieving the standards of quality.

PROBLEMS FROM MISAPPLICATION, UNDERSTANDING CONTEXT

I do not wish to suggest that there is anything intrinsically wrong with the various concepts and systems, but rather that problems can and do develop in the misapplication of the programs and systems.

For example, the attempted installation of an MRP system in a company for which its market, product line, and other factors are not suited is not likely to work. Indeed, those systems that can operate with little or no inventory have little need for inventory storage and elaborate (computer) programs to manage inventory.

Similarly, there are some processes that should not be automated for practical and economic reasons. The important thing is understanding the context in which one or more of the tools would be useful in upgrading the productivity of the operations.

Each development program can be viewed as providing a "quantum-jump" for the business—a kind of higher energy state. The steps in refinement can continue in the life cycle of the business, starting from its origin to wherever the technology, management, and the market take it. Two important considerations include the selection of the particular area for development and the specific application that is appropriate at that time for the business or industry.

To those who have worked or are working toward the factory of the future with: (*a*) MIS (Management Information Systems), (*b*) CIM (Computer Integrated Manufacture), or (*c*) XXX (your own hybrid), I suggest that the cases presented are not just yesterday's problems, but that they can be viewed as virtually inevitable in business life cycles and that the need for development will continue with new and emerging industries and even established businesses that do not continually upgrade their systems.

NEED FOR CONTINUOUS DEVELOPMENT, USE OF SERVICES

As described in the previous paragraph, characteristic problems can recur, and therein lies the value of the material presented. Even quality control, the foundations of which were developed in our country, is being rediscovered across the land.

Two programs are shown in which supporting service, working along with plant personnel, was utilized. These programs developed to fulfill a need. Some organizations also conduct fixed-format programs. Care should be exercised in considering fixed-format programs to assure that the program is appropriate for the situation. Another form of services, process consulting, is a sort of "coach and guide" role in an organization.[2]

Although there are a number of problems that a person providing consulting services cannot solve, there are also some problems (often not visible to management) in which the independent status and mandate provide an opportunity to uncover and resolve special problems. An example of this is a situation in which one department needs but cannot get information from another department. With care, the informational needs can be met and more effective ways of operating can be introduced.

The qualified industrial analyst is knowledgeable both about human behavior and the complexity of operating systems. In this respect, the analyst does not readily project the problems of a system on to the manager. This is because the analyst knows that people in their various roles may be constrained by local conditions or external factors beyond the scope of their capability to change or control.

If a situation in the various cases presented does not seem to be "right," the reader might bear in mind that each person has to deal with things as they are at the time. A person may feel a slight frustration by a deficiency in the organization, but an untimely restructuring of the staff may, in some cases, exacerbate the situation at a time when some level of control is necessary to resolve other immediate operating problems. Similarly, if an operating system restricts actions that should be undertaken, this may be the tipoff that the system should be upgraded.

While each chapter is developed around a leading subject such as productivity or quality control, a discussion or reference to closely related topics is also given, especially where it is important to present a comprehensive picture of the context and development. Out on the factory floor, simultaneous actions take place and most events are interrelated. Thus, for example, a reference to a term like *quality* or *material control* will appear in those chapters where the subjects are related parts of the general program presented.

FORMAT OF MATERIAL, CHAPTER SUBJECTS

To provide a distinction between the regular text and the narrative programs, the regular text is typeset with standard margins, using 11-point type, while the narrative programs are presented with indented margins using 10-point type.

This book covers applications in maufacturing engineering and manufacturing management systems. Chapters 2 through 7 deal with the details of each program. While the specific technical tools that were utilized are presented, this does not imply that one can lift and transplant a solution verbatim. The approach for each situation must be determined by the context of the problem. However, one can gain an understanding of the process and methods that were employed.

SYSTEM ANALYSIS, DESIGN, AND SYNTHESIS

In broad terms, each program presented employs the elements of system analysis, design, and synthesis as applied to the particular problem or need. The general steps include:

- Definition of the problem and scope of study.
- Statement of objectives and criteria of effectiveness.
- Documentation and functional analysis of macro and subsystems.
- Development of alternative plans and concepts.
- Selection, installation, and prove-in of new system or process.

There is an array of tools at the disposal of the engineer or manager, many of which are illustrated in the various programs. In the course of the development work, inconsistencies and obsolete procedures will be uncovered. The task is to present clear and useful representations of sometimes complex and/or ambiguous procedures. When these are revealed—the solution is often evident.

In development work, as noted earlier, the approach is as important as the content. If the people involved in the change are treated with good interpersonal relationships, the new system is more likely to work well.

Chapter 8, on advance manufacturing planning, presents a conceptual synthesis on automation. Chapter 9 presents material on management and technology, including a discussion of management concepts as well as material on analytical tools and techniques.

The value of the material is in learning about characteristic experiences in problem areas, and in acquiring the knowledge about development programs that improve productivity and quality. The narrative accounts are presented with fictional companies, products, names, and locations. If you see something familiar, it is because the situations described happen in many organizations. I am reminded of C. Northcote Parkinson, author of "Parkinson's Law," who told the tale of an American industrialist who called him up to inquire how he knew what was going on in his plant.[3]

MANUFACTURING PRODUCTIVITY AND ECONOMIC VITALITY

As noted earlier, some companies exhibit a high degree of productivity and product quality. However, there is a need to improve the general productivity of American industry. The data[4] from the Bureau of Labor Statistics for the more recent years show that there is no stable or upward trend in manufacturing productivity for the United States. The production of high-quality consumer products is important. But when one considers that an *improvement in manufacturing productivity is the driving engine of economic vitality,* the task takes on a more compelling significance. The following chapter will discuss the subject of productivity in more detail.

MANUFACTURING ENGINEERING

If at least one of the imperatives[5] described in *Made in America* by the MIT Commission on Industrial Productivity is acted upon, there will be an increased focus on manufacturing and the production process. And in a closely related reference,[6] The National Academy of Engineering draws attention to "the emerging emphasis on manufacturing engineering." This book focuses on industrial and manufacturing engineering and its role in manufacturing development. Engineers, managers, educators, and those in government all have a role in the larger economic and social picture. The challenge is there!

CHAPTER SUMMARY

To meet the promising challenges for American industry in the 1990s, managers, engineers, and workers in notable companies are engaged in bringing about innovative changes in the way business operates. Strategic changes in manufacturing operations are taking place. The subject matter of this book presents the characteristic experiences of people in manufacturing who are working on significant problem areas, and the subsequent development programs that have taken place to improve manufacturing productivity and product quality.

The subjects of personnel matters, management style, and worker involvement are recognized as very important components of developing effective operations. The applications presented here focus on the technical aspects of manufacturing engineering and manufacturing management systems.

The general steps in development programs include:
- Definition of the problem and scope of study.
- Statement of objectives and criteria of effectiveness.
- Documentation and functional analysis of macro and subsystems.
- Development of alternative plans and concepts.
- Selection, installation, and prove-in of new system or process.

When one considers that an improvement in manufacturing productivity is the driving engine of economic vitality, the task takes on a very compelling significance. There are indications of an increased focus on manufacturing and an emerging emphasis on manufacturing engineering.

CHAPTER 2

PRODUCTIVITY

IMPORTANCE OF PRODUCTIVITY, PRODUCTIVITY CENTERS

The importance of productivity to the economic well-being of a nation is recognized throughout the world. Many countries have organized "productivity centers." These organizations and institutions are charged with the responsibility of developing and fostering policies and practices to improve the output of their people and the effective utilization of their resources. In the United States, in addition to governmental agencies, various centers exist in universities, technical societies, and commercial organizations that prepare and distribute material on the subject of productivity.

PRODUCTIVITY, DEFINITION, RATES

Productivity can be defined as the ratio of output to input. As applied to a manufacturing company, the output may be expressed in units produced or sales dollars, while the input may be expressed as labor, material, and/or capital costs.

In recent years, there have been some notable success stories on the productivity of some U.S. industries, but the general trend has not increased. For the United States, the multifactorial productivity increase (a composite measure of the effectiveness of labor and capital inputs) has dropped from close to 2 percent in the period from 1948 to 1973 to less than a 1-percent increase in the period from 1979 to 1986.[1]

In the same relative periods, the rate of increase in labor productivity has declined from about 3 percent to about 1.5 percent. By comparison, the productivity increase of other countries ranges from over 2 percent to 5 percent.[2] The manufacturing productivity increase for the United States in 1990 was at 2.6 percent and is reported at an average of 1.9 percent for the first, second, and third quarters (-1.8, 3.7, and 3.8 respectively) of 1991.

FACTORS AFFECTING PRODUCTIVITY

The actions taken within several different sectors of society, including business, government, educational systems, and union organizations, can bring about an increase in our national productivity.

Most certainly, the driving force for improvement of productivity should originate from corporate leadership and the application of progressive management. The execution of development falls largely to engineers in product design, machine design, and manufacturing engineering.

Other important factors include: the support of productivity goals on the part of employees, whether unionized or not; the quality of education, which has a bearing on the effectiveness of the men and women who enter the work force; and finally, the strategic and legislative actions of government, which also affect industrial productivity. Fiscal and monetary policies may also affect the productivity index, but these aspects are beyond the scope of this book.

To expand on the previous paragraph without getting into details beyond the focus of manufacturing development, I would like to offer a few additional comments on the general aspects of productivity. Corporate leadership means, among other things, formulating policy to reflect long-range goals and development. Specifically, this includes investment in the now commonly called "world-class" perspective for products, production, marketing, and sales. The application of progressive management means sensitivity and responsiveness to new approaches and applications in various areas, including manufacturing development.

In the social dynamics of some industrial organizations there are implicit adversarial relationships between labor and management. The concerns of unions and management, if viewed in the form of Venn diagrams, may be represented as two partially intersecting circles. Where the shared concerns are in support and active pursuit of productivity, experience indicates that all in the organization benefit.

The federal regulations of business and industry also affect productivity. For example, the IRS regulations on capital depreciation affect the rate at which machine tools can be amortized. In most instances, shorter capital depreciation rates would reflect the realities of operational and technical obsolescence and would provide an incentive to replace outdated machinery with more productive equipment.

The value and effect of the educational level of those entering the workplace cannot be overemphasized. There are many benefits, but certainly the prospects for productivity increase with well-educated employees at all levels.

There is no singular or easy way to increase productivity. The components of a given task or body of work to be performed can be studied and analyzed in minute detail to obtain the best method for the task. Output, however, may vary considerably, depending upon many factors. There is not even a simple relationship between morale and productivity.[3] The development of manufacturing operations, however, is a good starting place. Thus we begin with the first narrative.

NARRATIVE: HITECH MACHINE COMPANY

Driving north on Interstate 95 through the New England countryside, Mark experienced some anxiety about taking over the position of manufacturing manager for the HiTech

Machine Company. As he examined his feeling he knew this anxiety did not relate to his capabilities; but instead, it was based upon a comment he had heard about the native New England mindset, "They like things as they are; don't try to change things." But changing things would be a consequence of the developmental work for which he was hired!

Mark thought about his first visit to the plant. He had met with the president, the heads of sales and engineering, and the company controller, along with several people in manufacturing. During his tour of the facilities, Mark noted a fairly extensive engineering department. His observations of manufacturing indicated that much development work was necessary.

During Mark's subsequent meeting with Everett, the president, he was told, "I want you to improve the productivity of our manufacturing operations. As you know, we are expanding into several new product lines and are becoming a growth industry, but we have to get costs in line! You will, of course, be sitting in with our officers in the management meetings."

Background

The company started as a small tool and die shop serving nearby industries, and as business grew, it undertook major machine orders. Some of the equipment required precision XY-coordinate-locating electronics along with the machine tools. The engineering department had added a substantial number of new engineers to design the new machines and electronic controls. Additional people were also brought into the sales staff to widen the customer base and meet the customer service demand.

The company had recently taken the current name, HiTech Machine Company, to reflect the growing high-tech product line. As more space was required for engineering, manufacturing, sales, and accounting, operations were set up in several different buildings, wherever space could be found. The personnel level had grown to over 400 people, and some overtime work was being performed to try to catch up with the demand against falling productivity.

Improving Productivity

Thus, Mark undertook his role as manufacturing manager and his special assignment to improve productivity. Arriving at the plant fairly early, he entered his office and noticed a stack of memos on a corner of his desk. He scanned the most recent memos and then went on to study the schedule and production report for the current month. The report showed a growing backlog on the new line of XY-machine tools. The production-cost report, which had just arrived from accounting, showed a rise in the regular production costs. Mark could see that business was good, but he had to get costs under control.

Having seen enough of the production figures, Mark left his office to talk with the production supervisors and to gain a more detailed understanding of the workflow throughout the plant. In his discussions with each supervisor, Mark occasionally raised questions as a means of testing his understanding of the situation or problem under discussion.

During this early period, you could almost say that Mark wasn't doing anything, except, of course, taking care of matters that required prompt action. As a manager, Mark thought about his role in the company—about what he could contribute in support of corporate goals.

In the following weeks Mark made periodic visits to each operating section and continued to talk with each supervisor about operations in their areas. In the course of the meetings, the statements from the supervisors of each section were as follows:

Machine shop: "We don't have any problems, well—ah, we could use one of those new NC milling machines like I saw at the trade show. It could help us get the work out and hold the tolerances better."

Electronic shop: "We are having some technical problems. I can take care of them, but then our production falls off when I'm troubleshooting. Sometimes I can get the product engineer to solve them, but he's usually too busy on new-product design."

Final assembly: "We are experiencing some extra work because we can't get all the parts to complete an assembly. Then we have to set the job aside and chase the parts."

Production control: "We're trying to improve our material control. Maybe we should consider a computer system. One other item: I can't get engineering to specify a disposition of old parts when they come up with a new design. Having all these parts—some old, some new—is causing problems in filling parts requisitions and finding storage space."

Purchasing: "We are trying to get quantity discounts, but on some of the new electronic parts, the requirements aren't high enough."

Tool shop: "We have been rebuilding some of our jigs and fixtures because some of the new parts don't fit properly in the older tools. Maybe we should replace some of the original tooling."

Tool design and methods: "Engineering keeps sending us changes over the current design release. We're seeing extra work in design revisions of tools and process sheets."

Receiving and shipping: "With the increased number of trucks coming in here, we don't have enough truck docks and service bays to handle the work. In the winter, snow blows all over the dock area and we have a hard time moving the equipment."

Inspection department: "Our electronics inspector has been dividing his time between here and our other two shops downtown on Maple Street. But with the time lost in going between the buildings and the increased workload, we may soon need another inspector."

Following the talks with the supervisors, Mark expressed his thanks for their responses. He told them that he would be following up with them on the various tasks along with the regular work.

During the informal talks with members of the production department to solicit comments about problem areas, he knew it would be something like opening Pandora's box, but he wanted to evaluate each person's response as an indication of how each viewed his or her job. He also wanted to provide employees with the opportunity to voice their problems and to convey the feeling that he would support them in their work.

At this point there is a clearer picture of the situation in the plant and some of the problems that faced the new manufacturing manager. The reader may anticipate some of the matters to be pursued more closely. This is how the program developed:

Returning to his office, Mark asked the department secretary to call a department meeting for 11:30. The agenda was to include production level, productivity, and current action items. While Mark was reviewing the personnel file of his department staff, he received a call from Steve, the vice president of sales. Steve wanted to know about the shipping date on the new R-7 controller. Mark mentioned that he would get back to him with the information.

Mark opened the department meeting with the following remarks: "The first topic on the agenda is the production level. I note from this month's production report that we are doing pretty well in keeping up with the schedule. We should, however, anticipate some increases in production requirements. The current sales forecast I have just received shows an expected 7-percent increase in demand. I mention this because it may affect the production schedule. Any adjustment in the schedule will be distributed to you.

"On the next item, productivity—you all know about some of the new product lines and how these have affected our regular production. The current performance report from accounting shows some production-cost increases. A share of this increased cost is to be expected in setting up the new product lines. However, along with the new developments and production increases, we still have to maintain our productivity. I'll have more to say about the subject of productivity in the coming weeks. I'll be sitting down with each one of you to talk some more about current needs and problems. Are there any questions at this time?"

The members were a little reluctant to talk in the department meeting about problems, but finally, the supervisor of shipping and receiving spoke up: "Can we talk about a current order problem?"

"Yes, of course!" Mark responded.

"Well," continued the shipping supervisor, "a customer has been calling me about a shipping date on the new R-7 controller. We don't have the cables for the unit."

At that point, John, the supervisor of final assembly, spoke up: "I have asked engineering for the pin-out configuration for the cable. As soon as we get it we can make up the cables."

"John, would you follow up on this," Mark responded, "and let us know this afternoon so we can firm up the delivery date?"

"Are there any other urgent matters?" Mark asked. Hearing none, he expressed his thanks and adjourned the meeting.

In the following days, Mark began to formulate his ideas about the situation in the company. In his mind, he was starting to separate the symptoms of problems from their basic causes. He saw several kinds of problems including structural, staffing, and system. There were also long-range needs, such as an integrated facility, but planning for that was not possible at this time.

In the course of Mark's regular work he met with the managers of sales, engineering, and accounting. During a meeting with Steve, the sales manager, Mark inquired about the new sales forecast. Steve assured him, "The business is there, if our company can deliver."

There were a number of things to go over with Ed, the vice president of engineering. When Mark inquired about updating the engineering-change system, Ed responded, "Yes, I understand we have some problems there. I'll be glad to work with you on it."

Mark switched the subject to the forthcoming management meeting by saying, "I'm planning to set up a formal manufacturing engineering group to deal with the growing technical needs in manufacturing.

"Manufacturing has not kept up with the pace of new-product design and the growing sales demand. Some of the problems develop in this way: The advance product-design group gets going in the lab with especially selected parts, 'breadboarding' and tweaking-up all of the components until the system works. Then the salespeople get hold of the design and sell a prototype model.

"To produce the product, manufacturing has to use commercial parts and line operators to build the units. We need to develop the manufacturing technology so that the products can be made in our production shops. We have to do a better job of manufacturing planning, tooling, and shop service."

Mark smiled and continued to look at Ed, saying, "Your engineering groups are producing new product lines for us and business is good, but manufacturing is not yet in a position to deal with the new technology. I know we're faced with leadership in the marketplace, and to provide this we need to establish a higher capability in industrial and manufacturing engineering. I'll be bringing this up in our management meeting. Could I have your views on this?"

Ed paused a moment, then responded, "Basically, I agree with your analysis. Some of our product design time is taken up with manufacturing problems. In general, I agree; you need manufacturing engineers."

In the meeting with the controller, Mark opened up the subject of production cost. He requested that accounting come up with a special "new-line setup" charge. The purpose was to identify the cost of a new-line setup apart from the regular production cost. Harriet, the controller, responded, "Yes we can do that, but be sure your people use the charge properly."

The management meeting was scheduled for 10:00 in the paneled boardroom. Mark was ready. Everett, the president, opened the meeting with the remarks, "I'm glad to note that sales are up, and the new product line is coming along. Would each of you just give us the highlights of your reports so we can have adequate time for Mark's presentation of the

FIGURE 2–1
Development Program

1. Establish Manufacturing Engineering Function
   - Manufacturing planning, shop support, and ongoing cost reduction
2. Upgrade Operating Systems
   - Material control: Introduce JIT
   - Workflow/layout: Form and integrate manufacturing and assembly work cells
   - Reduce or eliminate setup time
   - Manufacturing design review procedure
   - Engineering change notice
3. Install Higher-Productivity Machine Tools and Initiate Preventive Maintenance Program
4. Support and Extend Quality-Control Program
5. Set Up Training Program for New and Reassigned Operators

---

productivity program I asked him to prepare?" In succession, each department report was presented. There was only an occasional question on one or two items of each report.

Everett turned to Mark, saying, "Mark, you've been with us only a short time, but, as you know, the special assignment is of considerable importance to us. Will you present your productivity development program?"

Mark stepped up to the easel that held the flip-sheets on the program. Turning back to look at the group, Mark started with, "Thank you. As you know, manufacturing is tooling up for the new product lines. At the same time, the production volume is increasing, and this, along with manufacturing development, should lead to production economies.

"In the program I am about to present, some of the things we can do, and some things we are undertaking with our present staff. But I submit to you that the greatest increase in productivity will come from some investment, the cost of which should be recovered through production savings. I will present more specifics on the kinds of investments as we proceed."

With that, Mark flipped the cover sheet of the tablet revealing the outline of his presentation as shown in Figure 2–1. Opening his telescopic pointer, he called attention to the first item on the program.

Establishing a Manufacturing Engineering Function

Proceeding, Mark stated, "Let's take each step in the program, starting with the section, 'Establish Manufacturing Engineering Function.'" Mark continued, "To meet the manufacturing requirements for the growing complexity and technology of our newer product lines, we need to establish a capable manufacturing engineering function. While we have a methods section that prepares process sheets, we need a full-scale industrial and manufacturing engineering function. The purpose of this is to be able to provide effective manufacturing planning and support to production operations. In addition, cost reduction should be viewed as one of the regular functions.

"We have one or two candidates in our shops who may make good manufacturing process planners, and in time I shall explore the possibilities. To head the manufacturing engineering function, however, we need to bring in a well-qualified engineer for the job."

Stepping back from the easel, Mark continued in a more informal tone, "If you'll permit a slight digression to emphasize the changed needs—Joe Smitt, the foreman of our machine shop, in reminiscing about the early days can recall when a drawing would just call for a bearing and he had to select and chase around for something that would work.

"While our shops have skilled people for conventional machine work, and the process sheets exist, the planning and layout for our high-tech product lines require an increased capability in manufacturing engineering."

Moving back toward the easel, Mark mentioned, "The details of each part of the development program including costs and savings will be presented in a separate report to the executive committee."

Upgrading Operating Systems

Mark continued: "On the next step in the program, it is evident that operating systems affect productivity. Upgrading several elements of our operating systems will help in this direction. We shall be reviewing our material control in the light of current operating needs and some of the newer options. Considerations are being given to some form of a computerized material control system. Our main thrust, however, is closer control and reduction of inventory through introduction of JIT and the bin/card reorder system.

"Indications are that we are carrying some excess and/or obsolete inventory, both WIP (work-in-process) and finished goods. A sample check of parts and work orders shows that we have some inactive items held in stock for up to five years and that some questionable work orders have been on the books for several years. It is obvious that we must take a look at our entire material control system."

At the turn of this discussion, Harriet, the controller, readjusted her position in her chair. Evidently she was very interested in the financial aspects of a potential adjustment to the dollar value of the inventory account.

Improve Work Flow

As Mark placed his pointer on the next item in the program, he continued, "We plan to reduce materials handling and improve the workflow by realignment and relayout of some of our operations. In a cursory walk through our shop it may not be evident, but a good share of the material gets transported back and forth from several work centers until it reaches final assembly. This not only increases production cost, but it also affects our potential material control options as to processing and inventory position.

"Our plan is to apply group technology analysis to determine the design/process family groups of parts. With this knowledge we can then arrange the machines in manufacturing cells to process the family of parts. Ultimately each work cell will be arranged to improve workflow in our main plant. While we cannot entirely eliminate the handling between the several buildings at present, we should initiate a long-range consolidation plan. As part of the program, we also plan to reduce or eliminate setup time."

Focusing his eye contact toward Steve and Everett, Mark went on, "The next item under systems development concerns our ability to get products to the market quickly and at competitive costs. We are preparing a proposal for a manufacturing design review procedure.

"Essentially, the procedure is to provide a mechanism for review of new part and product designs by the responsible manufacturing engineer before the design is formalized and released to manufacturing. This will include provision for an initial modification or design change that will shorten production time and/or reduce manufacturing cost. Of course, any suggested changes will be subject to the approval of the responsible product design engineer. I shall be reviewing the proposal with Ed in the near future."

Mark proceeded with, "The next item, although relatively minor, is upgrading our engineering change notice (ECN) procedures. Production control (or as generally called, material control) is requesting the disposition of old parts when product engineering comes up with replacement parts. Among other things, the accumulation of old parts affects both storage and operating plant space, which are at a premium. I have discussed the changes with Ed, and the procedure is being reviewed. The procedure will also be presented to accounting for their review and approval."

At this point Everett spoke up, "Mark, if this is a convenient place to break, I suggest we take a few minutes and have some coffee brought in." During the break, Harriet collared Mark to express her interest in the inventory review when it is completed.

As the last person reentered the conference room and sat down, Mark proceeded, "I'll try to move along here. As you may realize, elements of this program are in various stages of development. Whatever requires special authorization will be detailed and forwarded to the executive committee as noted earlier."

Install More Productive Machine Tools

Mark continued, "The next item concerns the installation of more productive machine tools. We have recently installed a new component-insertion machine, and the pilot run shows a cost saving over the previous process. However, we have a large number of conventional milling machines with the associated tooling for various job setups that we do. In reviewing the operations with Joe, our machine shop foreman, we feel that we have the potential to reduce setup time, costs, and plant space by replacing several of the millers with one NC (numerical control) vertical miller. An economic analysis has been initiated. In addition, we plan to initiate a preventive maintenance program to help maintain quality and reduce random machine failures."

Support Quality Control Program

"There is a tradition in the machine shop," Mark went on, "that each machinist is responsible for the quality of his or her own work. This is an attitude—pride in one's work—and a practice that I would not want to change! If you look over the inspection reports, the work coming out of the shop shows hardly any rejections. However, as the company expands, our shop service staff is being called upon to help production operators solve equipment problems when the process gets out of control. In this respect, we wish to be in a position to support and extend a quality control program, as a comprehensive operating business policy."

Set Up Training Program

Mark moved on to the last item, "One of the means to maintain and support our quality level is to set up a training program for new and reassigned operators. This would provide for the opportunity to welcome new employees, explain procedures, and develop a sense of pride and identity with HiTech Machine.

"Special training would be provided as needed. We are experiencing the need for training of operators in electronic assembly on how to handle sensitive CMOS (complementary metal-oxide semiconductor) chips, soldering equipment and techniques, grounding requirements, and the like. This kind of program has the support of our personnel supervisor, Clarence, who feels it would help attract good employees to our company."

With that, Mark added, "Thank you," and then proceeded to close the telescoping pointer, after which he inserted it in his suit jacket.

Everett promptly spoke up, "Thank you, Mark. You have presented a comprehensive program. We shall look for the hard copy of your report. Since we are running short of time, I'm going to ask that we hold all questions until we meet again to review the program." As the meeting adjourned, the members rushed out to attend to other matters. Mark went out into the shop to follow up on a production problem.

In time, the formal proposal on the development program was submitted to the executive committee. The formalization of the manufacturing engineering function was approved along with a job requisition for an engineer to head up the function.

Working with personnel and other appropriate departments, Mark selected a candidate to head up the newly created position in manufacturing engineering. The engineer was well qualified, with seven years of successful experience in the field and an educational background in science and industrial engineering. From Mark's standpoint, the candidate selected would also be a promotable employee.

Mark spent some time with Dan, the new head of manufacturing engineering, to introduce him to the manufacturing staff and the managers of other departments. While Dan was highly trained in his field, he was also a very people-oriented person—a very important character trait in his field. Dan could see the opportunity to "make a contribution to company operations" in his new position by improving manufacturing productivity.

After the introductions and a tour of the plant, Mark led Dan back into his office. Mark invited Dan to sit down, saying, "As I explained, prior to your arrival we initiated a development program to improve the productivity of manufacturing operations." Handing Dan a copy of the

Development Program, Mark went on, "In addition to your regular work, I would like you to pursue the various elements of this program. Check with me on any questions you may have, and keep me informed on the progress of the work."

Then Mark stated, "There is a special task I would like you to undertake right away. We are experiencing problems in the lay-up of the large planar-grid assemblies in the Maple Street building. Would you look at the operation and see if you can straighten it out?"

Dan responded, "Thank you, I'll get on it," and he left the office to undertake the assignment.

Investing in Manufacturing Engineering

As the narrative continues, some of the specific things that were done in developing manufacturing will be described. However, the very specific things—though informative and, hopefully, interesting—are not the message! (The specific measures required to upgrade any process will depend upon the specific process.) Indeed, the message and significance of this chapter is that development took place in manufacturing, and that it was brought about by investing in manufacturing engineering and manufacturing technology, from which improvement in productivity developed!

The presence of general conditions and the criteria for good management and successful operations are, of course, important and essential. It can be argued that the existence of management excellence would, as a consequence, have ultimately undertaken the steps required to improve productivity. That's sometimes true, but in the real, imperfect world, all of the conditions for successful operations are not always present or perceived.

In past decades, we have passed through eras of exaggerated emphasis on one or more functions of industrial operations. Recall, for example, the stylistic emphasis on "fins" in car designs. In management, one can be guided by the model of Peters and Waterman, in the "McKinsey 7-S Framework,"[4] or the structure and principles of other writers on the subject. However, I suggest that in the functional divisions of industrial management, *a balanced approach is required*. This certainly includes *attention to excellence in engineering, both in product design and in manufacturing technology.*

This leads us back to the narrative, where investment in manufacturing technology was taking place. Dan was about to work on a manufacturing problem in the plant.

Dan briefly reviewed the process sheet for the planar grid, then drove down to the Maple Street building. Locating the supervisor of production in that work center, Dan introduced himself and explained his mission. Mary, the supervisor, led Dan into the room where the planar grid was being fabricated and then introduced Dan to the two men laying up the assembly.

Before getting into the details, a few notes may be of interest on the use of planar-grid assembly. The planar grid was actually a subassembly of one of HiTech's digitizer systems. Once assembled, the grid is hooked up to the electronic components and connected to a computer. With operating software, a video output, and an operator, the system can be used to translate graphic (analog) information into digital form. There are many kinds of digitizers, and the technology is constantly being developed. Accuracies are of the order of ± 0.010 to ± 0.005 inch.

The planar grids and tooling looked more like a setup for a weaving operation. The process consisted of laying down a series of parallel wires over a glass plate along one axis and then repeating the process for the other coordinate axis over the existing wires. The planar-grid assembly and fixture is shown in Figure 2–2.

In order to obtain the proper spacing of the magnet wires, steel registration bars were attached to the table. The registration bars had V-shaped notches spaced ¼ inch apart along their lengths.

The outside edge of the whole fixture consisted of a rectangular railing made of ordinary Douglas fir 2 × 4s. The

FIGURE 2–2
Planar-Grid Assembly and Fixture

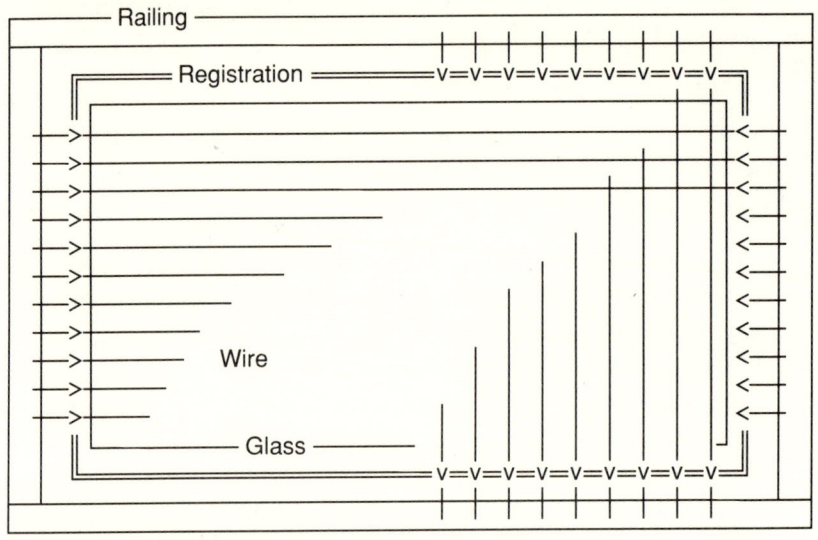

2 × 4 rails were supported at each corner of the fixture. The rails also had a series of steel dowel pins spaced at ¼-inch intervals to tie off each wire as it was strung.

The ¼-inch-thick glass plate, measuring 40 × 60 inches, was placed on the fixture and then aligned with the axis of the steel registration bars. The glass was then clamped to hold it in place.

In laying up the magnet wire, which was 0.0055 inch in diameter, an operator on one side of the fixture would first tie the free end of the wire to a pin in the rail, then pass the wire over the notch in the registration bar and send the spool of wire (held by an overhead pulley) over to the second operator on the other side of the table.

At this position, the second operator would grasp the wire, lay it in the proper V-groove, pull the wire tight, and then make it fast to the appropriate nail. In addition, the tension was increased on the wires with the use of rubber bands looped over each wire. The process would then be repeated, leading the wire back and forth, progressively laying up parallel wires on one axis. After one set of parallel wires was laid down on one axis, the process would be repeated for the other axis.

If any of the wires broke, which happened fairly often while the wire was being stretched, the wire would be removed, and another wire strung in its place.

The final step of this process was to bond the wires to the glass with a hot-melt glue, after which the wires along the outside edge of the glass were cut free of the fixture. The glass plate with the wire grid could then be removed from the fixture.

The process appeared simple enough—so what then was the problem? Planar-grid assemblies were often scrapped because they were unusable. Upon inspection, the grid wires were found to be out of position by up to 0.027 inch. This was far beyond the specification for the product and would have given erroneous output in the digitizer system.

Dan observed the process for a while and talked to the two operators about their work. This was just part of building a good working relationship. A phone call came in for Dan concerning a short meeting at the main plant.

The next morning, after thinking about the method of fabrication and tooling for this job, Dan had several ideas on the causes of the problems and how to upgrade the manufacturing process. Greeting the two operators, Bob and Mike, in the grid assembly room, Dan talked about the process.

Dan explained, "There are several things we can do to solve these problems. Some of the things have to do with the tooling and facilities. First let's talk about the fixture and this work area.

"The railing on the fixture is like a beam. It's supported, but not restrained, at two ends. When one wire after another is pulled tight and affixed to the beam, both the wires and the beam experience a change. Although each individual force is small (you remember we measured the force at $1/4$ pound), the result of the combined tensile forces of 240 wires is sufficient to bend the railing, which in turn affects the grid wires attached to it."

Both of the operators, Bob and Mike, listened with interest. One could sense they were experiencing something new here and liked the feeling of understanding the process better.

Dan continued, "We'll have the railing of this fixture supported throughout its length so that it doesn't bend. There is, however, a more significant and fundamental factor in the actual laying-up process."

Resuming, Dan said, "Try this when you lay down the grid wires, just draw the wire straight and allow it to slip through your gloved fingers while you loop the wire around the pin and finally secure it."

"You might be interested," Dan mentioned, "in understanding what happens. First, you have to realize that magnet wire is a 'ductile' material as opposed to an 'elastic' material like steel piano wire. In general, you can stretch steel up to its elastic limit and it will recover. But if you stretch magnet wire it will neck-down, thinning its diameter and become weaker and more subject to displacement. So, let's try the new process."

Bob and Mike readily adopted the new technique. First, the fixture was reinforced and measures were undertaken to provide a "clean room" for the assembly. Then attempts were made to regulate the temperature of the room in which the assembly was taking place. The purpose of this was to avoid a shift in the grid spacing due to thermal expansion or contraction of the registration bar and magnet wire.

At this point the reader interested in the details can review Dan's calculations on the sources of errors. And, for those more interested in the overall narrative, the thread of the story can be picked up just after the calculations.

In addition to the errors caused by stretching the wires, there were other factors. Dan's calculations on contributing sources of errors were as follows:

Deflection of Railing

The 2 × 4-inch railing, which was set on the diagonal, could be viewed as a beam with a uniform load. The beam could be taken as having free ends, since the connection at the corners was not very rigid. The magnet wires acted as a uniform load on the railing. While the magnet wires were ductile and could relieve some of the stress applied, the following calculation was made as an indication of the order of magnitude of the deflection of the rail:

Relationship for maximum deflection,[5] "f":

$$f = \frac{5Wl^3}{384EI}$$

where:

$W = wl$, total uniform load, (¼ lb. × 4/in.) × (60 in.)
l = Length of beam, 60 in.
E = Modulus of elasticity, 1,950,000 lb. per sq. in.
I = Moment of inertia, in this case, on the diagonal (I_c),[6] (1 ⅝ by 3 ⅝), 2.158 in^4

On evaluating the above expression, the maximum bending of the railing was calculated at .0400 inch. Even if the railing to which the wires were attached was bent by half of that amount during the assembly, some of the wires could be expected to be out of position on the glass plate.

Registration Change

A temperature change of 8 degrees Fahrenheit (as experienced in the room) would affect the length of the steel registration bar and thus the position of the grid alignment notches in the bar. The change in the length,[7] "l", was computed as follows:

$$l = LkT$$

where:

L = Length of bar, 60 in.
k = Coefficient of expansion,[8] .0000065
T = Temperature change, 8°F.

In evaluating this relationship, it is apparent that the registration bar would change its length by .0031 inch. This would affect the position of the registration notches that determined the position of the magnet wire. Needless to say, the magnet wire would also be affected by temperature changes.

Prior to the effort, particle sizes of .0025 could be found on the glass plate. This could lead to dislocation of grid wires on top of the plate.

The first planar grid produced with the new process emerged from the assembly room. By now, others in the building were aware of the activity. Steve, the sales manager, even dropped by to check up on how the work was coming. As the inspector completed the initial set of measurements of the grid, she passed a copy of the report over to Dan.

The initial set of 25 measurements revealed that the difference, or offset, between adjacent wires did not vary by more than ±.001 inch!

A second more comprehensive set of measurements was taken. The values for the average variation[9] $\bar{x}$, and the standard deviation[10] s, were calculated as follows:

$$\bar{x} = \frac{\Sigma x_n}{n}$$

$$s = \sqrt{\frac{\Sigma x^2 - n \bar{x}^2}{n - 1}}$$

where:

X's are data values
n represents the number of samples
Σ (sigma) means "sum of"

For the x-axis, the computation showed:

$\bar{x} = .0000$

$s = .0013$

For the y-axis, the computation showed:

$\bar{x} = .0001$

$s = .0012$

For all practical purposes, the technology was pressed to the limit of its capability for this given design. With these results, the production was well within the specification for the assembly. In addition, the new development had reduced the cost of this production—a step in gaining productivity.

New product-design concepts continually evolve for digitizers as they will for all products. Carrying the manufacturing technology of any given product design to the highest level of capability (within economic bounds) is certainly one of the prime goals of industrial and manufacturing engineering. In attaining the state of manufacturing "perfection," a share of the production can and often is performed by hand.

One might inquire about the design and construction of the original fixture. Several points are relevant. In today's fast-moving technology there is an intense pressure to get new products to the marketplace in a timely fashion. Production processes that are basically sound, that can be set up quickly and made to work, shorten the time in getting the product to the market. Further, specific product designs and technology are subject to rapid obsolescence. A combination of appropriate tooling coupled with operator skill can, in many cases, provide quick response and successful production.

Dan was understandably pleased with the results. In travels throughout the plant he noticed he was gaining recognition from workers as he moved about. It wasn't long before Mark called Dan into his office to go over further work.

By now Mark's office was filled with a lot of additional projects, drawings, and operating documents. Mark began, "Dan, that was a good piece of work down at the Maple Street building! Will you now work on the regular development program? I would also like you to go over our process lines here in the main plant."

Dan responded, "Thank you. I have updated the process sheets on the planar-grid assembly to incorporate the new procedure. Occasionally I will check back to follow up on the process."

Mark responded, "Good" as Dan turned to take up the new assignment.

In time, each element of the program was undertaken. Dan prepared a draft of the manufacturing design review procedure for Mark's review and approval. The engineering change notice was updated, and both procedures were accepted by management.

The tool design and methods group had completed an analysis of all of the work that was run on the present three vertical milling machines. A study was also made with a machinery firm that supplies NC (numerical control) milling machines to determine the equivalent work-output capability. The analysis showed that one NC milling center could provide the same annual output as the present three millers, with savings in labor, tools, and space sufficient to recover the cost of the investment in slightly over a year. Subsequently, the investment, a step in improving productivity, was authorized.

Production space was recovered with the installation of the NC miller and the removal of other obsolete equipment. This led to a relayout of the workflow in the plant, with an associated reduction in materials handling. Improved inventory and material control followed.

Dan completed his review of the process lines in the main plant. He, along with other members of his group, found and corrected manufacturing processes that needed realignment and upgrading. Throughout the development, an enthusiastic, can-do attitude prevailed in the organization.

Where problems existed with purchased parts and raw material, the responsible engineer and purchasing agent worked with vendors to help meet requirements and maintain control of incoming material and parts. With this activity, the program spanned from raw material to final assembly. And further, the sales department instituted a customer service program.

Within three months the overall productivity of HiTech increased by 14 percent. Mark subsequently obtained his vice presidency, and the reader can see Dan as the new manufacturing manager. The focus of Dan's current work is planning the consolidation of operations in a new, integrated facility that would further improve productivity.

The narrative has shown how one company went about improving productivity. The specifics will vary. In general, leadership of and support from top management are essential. Further, the pursuit of productivity is more effective when the programs are companywide and involve all levels and functions of the organization.

With a commitment to excellence, middle management and staff are empowered to execute needed programs. With responsive supervisors, improvements suggested by the work force are more likely to be acted upon and installed at the workplace. In time, increases in productivity will follow.

CHAPTER SUMMARY

Productivity is the ratio of output to input. The rate of productivity increase is a measure of the economic health of a country. There is a compelling need to increase productivity in the United States.

The driving force for improvement of productivity should originate from corporate leadership and the application of progressive management. The execution of development programs falls largely to engineers and managers in product design, manufacturing engineering, and operations.

Other important factors include: the support of productivity goals on the part of employees, whether unionized or not; the quality of education, which has a bearing on the effectiveness of the men and women who enter the work force; and finally, the strategic and legislative actions of government, which also affect industrial productivity.

Manufacturing productivity development programs include:

- Establishment of an effective manufacturing engineering function

Manufacturing planning, shop support, and ongoing cost reduction.
- Development of the operating systems
Material control, consideration of JIT, if appropriate.
Workflow/layout: group technology, integrate manufacturing and assembly work cells, reduce materials handling.
Reduction or elimination of setup time.
Integration of the product design and manufacturing engineering procedure for effective response.
- Installation of higher productivity machine tools by replacing obsolete facilities
- Support of total quality control programs
- Provision for effective training program for new and reassigned operators

CHAPTER 3

QUALITY

MACHINE CAPABILITY STUDY, BASIS AND VALUE OF QUALITY

This chapter, on the subject of quality, provides an illustration of what to do when a process is not in control. The application consists of a machine capability study. More generally, the basis for quality control lies in an *understanding* of the statistical nature of processes and a *commitment* to support an appropriate program throughout an organization. The value of an effective program lies in an increased return on investment and profitability. The application of quality control (QC) principles can be viewed as tools to this end.

In this chapter we will see a process in trouble—a situation that can and does occur at various times in manufacturing plants. No irreverence is intended to the well-managed companies with quality programs. It's just that you can't change the statistical nature of a process. An effective quality control program attempts to deal with the inherent variation by providing the conditions for regulation of output within the specifications of the product.

The pursuit of the ultimate in product performance involves pressing the limits of manufacturing capability. In these extreme cases where a process is operating at the "threshold of capability," the output is commonly tested, sorted, and marketed accordingly. The early production of floppy disks for computers was treated in this fashion.

The conditions for effective quality control involve many elements of a program. Following a commitment and general understanding, as mentioned earlier, other elements include: provision for a broad-based program, adequate staffing and equipment, training, and responsive integration with other company functions. Those who would like to pursue the subject beyond the material presented here are encouraged to avail themselves of the references[1] provided in the chapter notes.

The following narrative presents the background to this industrial tale along with the analysis of and solution to the problem.

NARRATIVE: CLEANPACK COMPANY

Process out of Control

Little plastic hand-cleaner packets, like the kind you get after a lobster dinner, were flopping all over the production conveyer—4 packets at a time, 240 packets every minute! The gears of the automated production machine were methodically driving the whole system, whether it was making a good product or not. The packets were sometimes cut in half, leaking cleaning solution all over the drive rollers. Rocker arms would jump after cutting the web at the wrong place. The machine seemed to be experiencing uncontrolled mechanical vibrations.

Operators down the line were busy in frantic efforts to shove the scrap packets in waste bins. None of the adjustments tried by the setup men would bring the machine back into regulation.

Clearly, production was not in control. The quality of the product fell to such a point that several of the production operators were given a temporary layoff until the machine could be brought back into control.

Background

An executive for one of the major food companies decided that he wanted to go into business for himself. Doug, the executive, could see a new market growing for the small disposable packets that could be used for cleaning your hands in a restaurant or on a trip. Doug knew the market and was a superb performer in the sales area.

After saying his goodbyes to his office associates, he proceeded to devote full time to setting up his new venture—the CleanPack Company. Earlier, he had contracted for the design of two completely automated fabrication and packaging machine systems to produce the small, handy cleaning packets.

Company Startup

Doug's initial efforts were devoted to developing the marketing plan and following up with the machinery designers and builders. Ultimately, about 12 months later, the two automated systems were installed in a new manufacturing building in a small Pennsylvania town. The operating staff was hired, and the machinery builders guided the initial prove-in of the production systems.

The Machine

The completely automated fabrication and packaging systems were a marvel of design. In some respects the systems were more complicated than a newspaper printing press. A schematic drawing of the identical systems is shown in Figure 3–1.

The process started with a wide sheet of foil that was fed from a continuous roll. The foil had a preprinted rectangular pattern, eight panels across (four front and four back panels). The foil was then slit lengthwise, separating front and back panels, to be joined later in the process after going through many convolutions around rollers in the automated system.

At the position where the front and back panels of the packets came together, a folded web saturated with a liquid cleaner was inserted into the middle of each panel just before being sealed.

FIGURE 3-1
Schematic Drawing of the Automated Production System

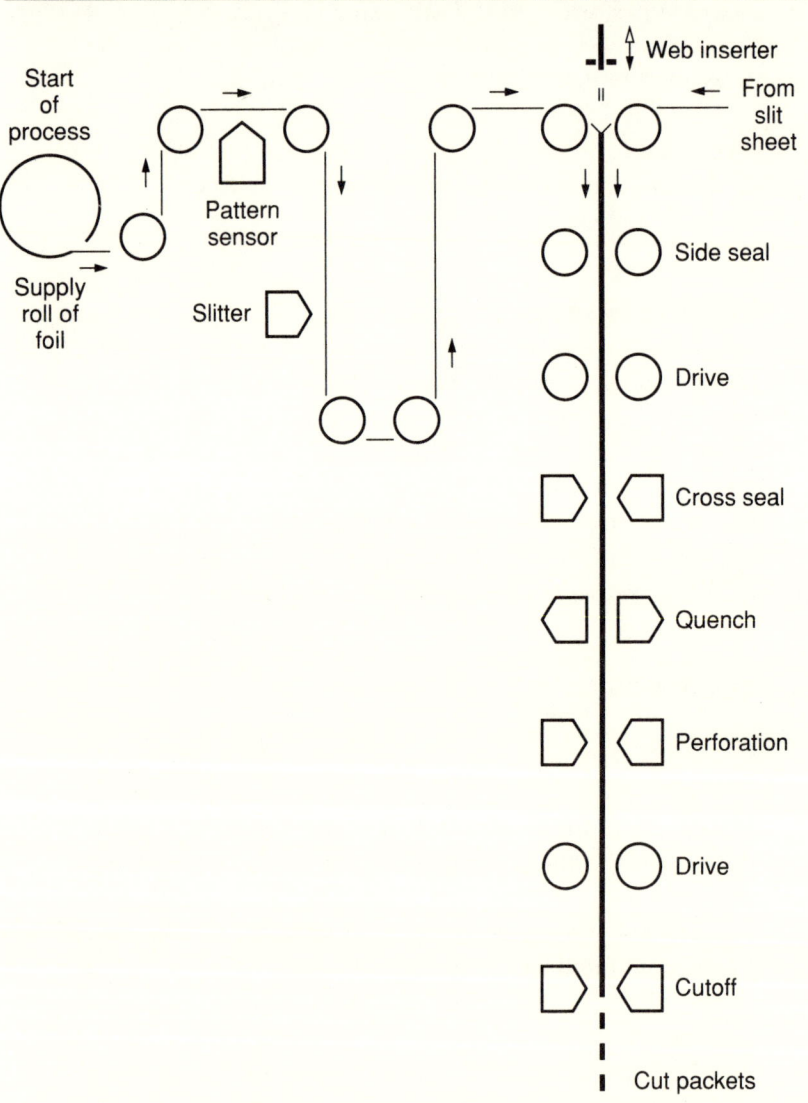

The front and back panels were ultimately sealed on all sides and subsequently perforated in order to separate each single packet. Four packets at a time emerged onto a conveyer belt for the final boxing by the line operators.

Statistical Control

As described in the beginning of this chapter, the process was out of control. The symptoms were evident. There was still a question about the lack of statistical *control. The significance of the term* statistical, *as used in the field of quality control, is that the variations that occur are due to pure chance—that is, there are no assignable causes. The usefulness of knowing whether or not a process is in statistical control will be brought out in the course of this material.*

Considerations

At this point, in a small company, with a process out of control, a general manager may be considering some of the following options:

1. *Solve the problem internally. Call a meeting with the staff to solve the problem, and/or hire an engineer for this and other needs.*
2. *Call the machine designers and builders to work on the problem.*
3. *Retain an engineering consultant.*

While the above considerations are taking place, a manager is also likely to order special control of finished-goods inventory so that critical orders can be filled. In addition, customers may be contacted over the impending delay in meeting delivery commitments. Finally, a manager may also think about the general reasons why the process got out of control and what steps should be taken to assure control in the future.

Limited Resources

Many small companies start out with limited resources in staff, equipment, and funds. To meet occasional needs for specialized service, they often turn to consultants for help in solving operating problems.

This provides for assistance without having a full-time commitment against limited funds. Such was the case here.

In taking stock of the situation, Doug, the president of the CleanPack Company, decided to seek supporting help. He called in an engineering consultant who he felt could analyze the problem and restore control to, and in, the automated process.

The following day, Clark, the consultant, arrived at the plant. Clark was introduced to Helmut, the plant manager, and his machine setup man, Karl. The group walked into the factory section to observe the operation of the automated production systems.

As noted earlier, there were two similar automated systems. For simplicity, we can call these Machine 1 and Machine 2. At the time of the visit, Machine 2 was completely shut down. The output of the machine was so far out of regulation that it was secured for major changes.

Machine 1 was in operation, however, so the process could be observed. For those interested in machinery and automated processes it was a sight to behold! From the beginning of the foil feed to the assembly and final rhythmic cutoff, all stations were synchronized to produce the 2 × 3-inch cleaning packets. While the machine was working, there were some product rejects and problems.

Clark made a few mental notes as he walked around the machine observing the process. He inquired, "Are there any drawings of the machine?" Helmut responded, "Ach, no!" Clark thanked Helmut and Karl for the tour and made arrangements for a following visit. Driving home that afternoon, Clark wondered where he would find one or more of the problems in this major automated system. But not knowing about the intricacies of the machine and its specific problems did not bother him. He knew he had to undertake a *machine capability study.*

Machine Capability Study

At this point it may be helpful to provide an explanation of a machine capability study *and how it relates to the subject of quality control.*

A machine designer who starts out to design a machine makes a lot of judgments about the physical configuration of the machine, its *elements, and the tolerances assigned to the fabrication of the parts. It requires a combination of creativity and the application of technical principles. Even a designer who gives it his or her "best shot" often cannot guarantee the performance of the machine—there are too many unknown variables. That's why prototypes are made, to test and then improve machine output.*

As applied to a production machine, the purpose of a capability study is to determine the character of the output. This output character refers to its statistical pattern, or distribution, including the measure of central tendency (like average) and the measure of dispersion (like range of values).

If the average value of a process and the variation (plus or minus) from the average fall within the permitted specification for the product, then the machine is capable of producing a product within the specifications. If the values exceeded the specification, then one would have to refine the machine to produce a closer distribution, and/or reconsider the specification of the product. (Selective assembly could also be employed, but that is beyond the focus of the objective here.)

The general purpose of a machine capability study is to determine whether or not a machine is capable of producing output within the specification. By comparison, the (nominal) objective of quality control is to maintain production within specification. And, as will be shown, a capability study can be used as a diagnostic tool to analyze processes that have gone out of control. Let's get back to the project.

> Clark called Helmut the next morning, before driving over to the plant, to verify that Machine 1 was operating. It was. In this second meeting, Helmut explained that the machinery design and fabrication company felt no further responsibility, since the machines were producing a good product during the installation, and the machines were accepted at that time.
>
> As the meeting progressed, Clark mentioned that it would be necessary to undertake a machine capability study. He explained that data would have to be collected in order to analyze the variables in the process. One of the leading variables is the cut length of the packets. When Clark asked Karl about the variation in the cut length of the packets, Karl reported: "about plus or minus $1/32$ of an inch."

Variables and Attributes

At this point, by way of background, note that parts or products can be inspected for either variables *or* attributes. *If a product is inspected for* variables, *it is inspected for quality characteristics that can be measured and expressed in numbers. An example of this is the measurement of the length of each packet produced from the machine. In the other case, quality characteristics can be observed as* attributes, *that is, by classifying them into one or two classes, usually defective or nondefective. An example of this, as applied to the CleanPack's product, is whether or not a packet leaks.*

While the cut length of the packets was not the only variable in this process, it was a good place to start. The reader will note that nothing has been said about the working elements of the machine, such as the gears, drive rollers, and other elements. In the project, the focus was on the output for what it could tell about the machine.

> Clark went on to explain that a series of consecutive samples from the machine would be needed for one continuous "hands-off" production run. The group, consisting of Helmut, Karl, and Clark, walked over to the operating line. Helmut explained to the operators that packets being produced from the machine would have to be collected. As the packets were collected, they were identified and accumulated in the order produced.
>
> Back in his office, Clark proceeded to measure the length of each packet with a micrometer. It may seem strange to measure a flimsy foil packet with a micrometer, but the reason and value will be clear when the graph of the measurements is observed.

In the following material, some project data and statistical formulas will be utilized. But the degree of detail is limited to the amount judged necessary for the reader to follow the concepts. A tradeoff of technical detail is made for ease in reading the material. However, technical correctness for all of the original data and computations is not sacrificed for convenience.

TABLE 3-1
Partial Data Set, Product Length, Machine 1

Piece Number	Length (inches)	Piece Number	Length (inches)	Piece Number	Length (inches)
1	3.011	5	2.987	9	2.999
2	3.014	6	2.998	10	2.987
3	2.989	7	3.009	11	2.953
4	2.969	8	2.986	12	2.964

Clark prepared a table of measurements, from which only a partial section is shown in Table 3–1. The table shows the piece number and its length.

After tabulating the measurements, there was no stopping. Working late, Clark went on to graph the data. After all, this was the exciting part—examining the statistical data for what they could reveal. A graph of the data is shown in Figure 3–2a. The plot showed a considerable variation. The reader can see the first piece was 3.011 inches long, the second piece was a trifle longer, the third piece was down to 2.989, the fourth piece was 2.969, and so on.

Preliminary Considerations

At this point in the analysis, the questions considered were:

- Does the graph look like a normal piece-by-piece variation?
- Is there a trend or anything unusual?

Somewhat bleary-eyed, Clark let his eyes play over the contours of graph. Was this one of Mandelbrot's fractals?[2] No. Was this a normal variation? No, not quite. There was something about it all taken together that did not look like a pattern from a random set of causes. The overall pattern seemed to snake up and down. It was then that Clark thought about adding a generalized envelope, (the dotted line) top and bottom, over the pattern as shown in Figure 3–2b.

The serpentine curve of the envelope led to the next question. What was the cause of the undulation of the envelope of the individual variations? In turn, this question

**FIGURE 3–2a
Pattern from Machine 1**

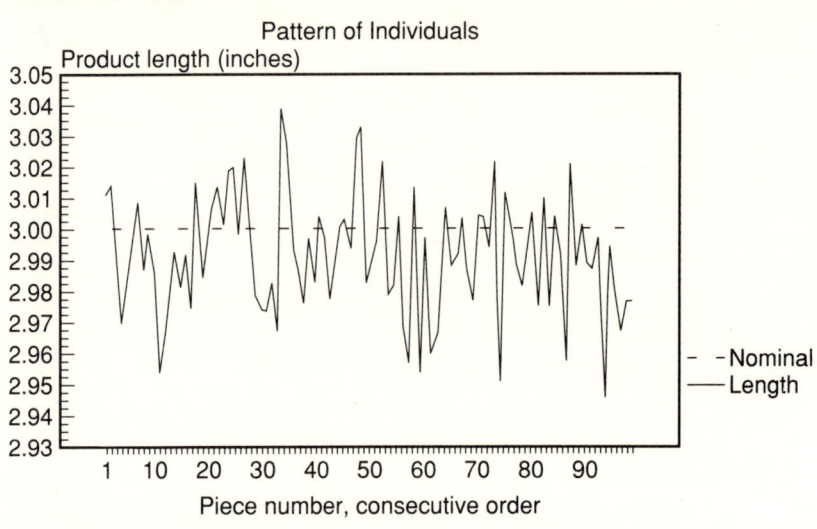

**FIGURE 3–2b
Pattern from Machine 1 with Envelope**

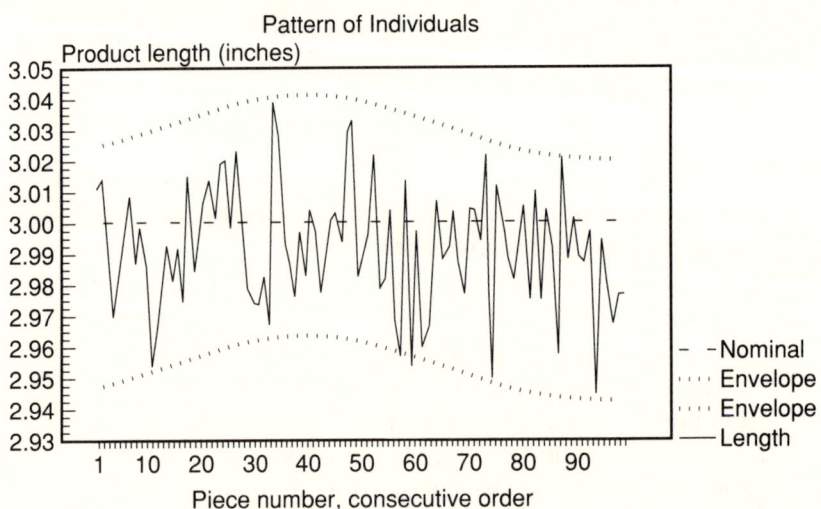

led to determining the periodicity of the envelope and, more specifically, the number of packet patterns between the highest and lowest points of the curve of the envelope.

From the graph, the number of patterns in line between the highest and the lowest points of the envelope were found to be 54 pieces. This was obtained from scaling the graph. What did this mean in relation to the automated production machine? Clark could hardly wait until he could get to the plant the next day to climb around the machine to find out what correlated to the number 54!

Fortunately, the next day, the machine was down. It was easy to count the number of patterns (packets) in the system. Counting backwards, starting from the end-cutoff position, the number of patterns were counted in the reverse order of each operating station in the machine. (To help visualize this, the reader may wish to refer back to the schematic drawing, Figure 3–1.)

There it was! There were exactly 54 patterns in line from the cutoff station to the packet- pattern- sensor station that controlled the packet cutoff! The machine had a feedback circuit that was always hunting for the "correct" position. The process was drifting above and below the nominal 3.000-inch cutoff setting.

The next obvious question was, why didn't the designers place the pattern sensor next to, or closer to, the cutoff station that it controlled? This was something to go over with the machinery designers.

Before engaging in a meeting with the designers, Clark went on to plot the distribution of the sample from Machine 1. The same data were used, as shown in the partial data set, Table 3–1. Using the first 50 measurements taken of the cut length of the packets, the graph of the distribution was plotted as shown in Figure 3–3.

As is commonly done, this graph was plotted by selecting convenient cell widths to show the characteristic distribution. Note that most of the packets (11 of 50) had a cut length at the mid-cell of 3.000 inches. On the whole, the process was fairly well centered. The variation or range, however, could be reduced by reducing the cause of snaking.

**FIGURE 3–3
Sample Distribution, Machine 1**

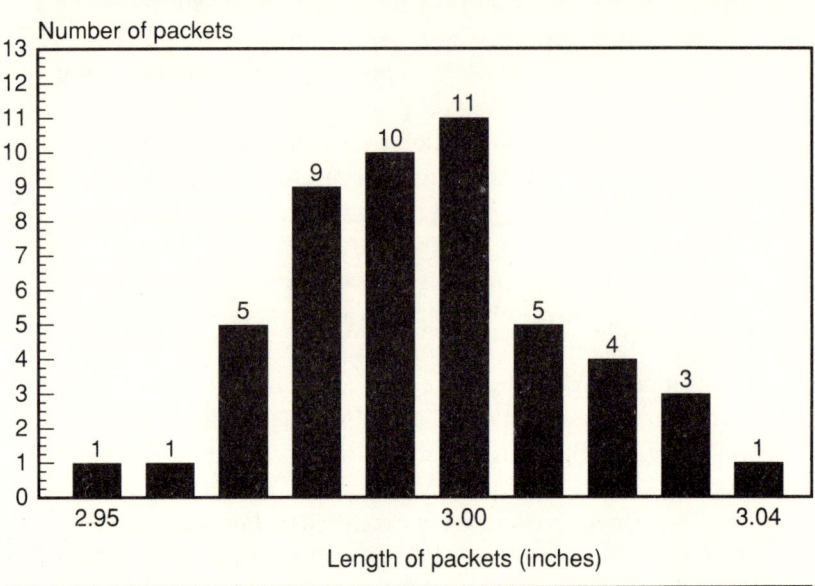

A capability study was also undertaken for the other machine. The data, graph, and results will be presented later in this chapter.

Helmut, the plant manager, made arrangements for a visit to the company that had designed and built the machine. The machinery design and construction company was located in a newly restored factory building just across the state line in New York. While driving north to the factory, Helmut and Clark got a chance to review some of the technical factors on the project.

After having coffee in the company conference room, the members of the group were introduced to a person named Nick, who could go over some of the technical aspects of the machine. Nick presented the basis of the design, and the expected packet cut-length variation as follows:

- The design was based upon maintaining tension on the foil.
- The machine employs feedback correction.

- The cut-length variation should be $\pm 1/32$ of an inch.

On closer questioning, Nick allowed that the cut length variation might be as high as $\pm 1/16$ of an inch.

Clark presented a record of the actual variation of the machines. Then the group reviewed the alternatives and came to agreement on steps to be taken to improve the performance of the machines:

1. Set up a standard black and white eye spot for the sensor. This is more effective than the pickup from the colored pattern on the foil.
2. Institute regular cleaning and maintenance as an essential requirement for proper machine performance. Cleaning the clutches is critical for proper regulation.
3. Check and maintain the quality of the foil in regard to its properties, including the precision and repeatability of the pattern.
4. Follow up on several other factors related to the tooling of the applicator and the moist web that is inserted into the packets.

Clark opened the subject of the location of the sensor that controls the final cutoff of the packets. After a long discussion, Nick agreed that, "moving the sensor closer to the cutoff station it controls, is not inconsistent with the design and its electronics." Recast, the statement can be translated to "It should improve performance."

The meeting adjourned, and members of the group were led into the shop to view a minor modification to one of their machines. After lunch, expressing thanks for the vendor's courtesy, Helmut and Clark headed south, back to the plant.

Earlier in this chapter, reference was made to the machine-design process. It is helpful to understand that designers tend to become committed to what has been set down on the drawing. It is just a natural feeling, as Mozart might have felt, who, when quizzed, asked, "Which note would you like me to change?"[3] (In Mozart's case, what note would you change!)

However, the performance of even a well-designed machine can often benefit from a fresh look and prove-in by other engineers. Sometimes the difference between a machine working well or not is as subtle as changing the coefficient of friction by adding a strip of Teflon at a critical place in the process. Often a sharp operator at the machine will come up with improvements in the process.

The following material presents computations of the average, standard deviation, and the total variation from sample data taken from 50 measurements of output from Machine 1.

First a word about statistical computations. In using relationships in statistics, there are some implicit assumptions regarding the use of sample data. In general, applications are based upon an assumed or reasonably appropriate use of the relationships for normal bell-shaped curve data. Beyond this, no elaboration is presented. As noted earlier, persons wishing to pursue the subject in more detail are referred to the references given in the chapter notes.

Calculation of Average and Standard Deviation

Using a common statistical hand-held calculator, Clark had entered the data from the first 50 measurements for Machine 1. He was seeking a preliminary index of the variation, even though the pattern and data did not indicate a (perfectly) normal distribution. The value for the average length was calculated as 2.995 inches, and the value for the standard deviation was calculated as 0.018 inch.

The average length is very close to the nominal 3.000-inch specification. This means that the calculated average value looks good. But, that is only half of the consideration.

As an example of why both statistical values are necessary, suppose two pieces of steel bar stock three inches long are needed. A piece of stock that is cut two inches long and a piece that is cut four inches long have an average length of three inches. But if the two-inch piece is too short, and the four-inch piece is too long for the intended use, then neither piece is useful. Information on the average value alone is insufficient to determine whether the pieces are acceptable. Calculation of the standard deviation is useful for this purpose.

Calculation of Range of Values (±3s)

Having calculated the value for one standard deviation (as a near-normal distribution index), the next step was to find the range of values for most of the output of the machine. (Plus and minus three standard deviations will include over 99 percent of the values.) The extreme packet lengths are calculated as:

$$2.995 + (3 \times 0.018) = 3.049 \text{ in., longest}$$
$$2.995 - (3 \times 0.018) = 2.941 \text{ in., shortest}$$

The total range, or variation, is:

$$6 \times 0.018 = 0.108 \text{ in.}$$

This range was in excess of the variation that was cited much earlier by Karl. (The computation was based on the first 50 samples. Had 100 samples been used, the standard deviation would have been even greater as the process shifted up and down from the centerline.)

Study of Machine 2

A similar analysis was performed for Machine 2. The data, pattern, and distribution were very different for this machine. A partial section of the data is shown in Table 3–2. Before the foil broke, 141 packets were collected. Only the last 100 measurements were plotted, since that is where the trouble started.

TABLE 3–2
Partial Data Set, Product Length, Machine 2

Piece Number	Length (inches)	Piece Number	Length (inches)	Piece Number	Length (inches)
1	3.004	5	2.991	9	3.014
2	3.023	6	3.052	10	3.029
3	3.013	7	2.984	11	2.988
4	2.980	8	2.978	12	3.025

FIGURE 3-4
Pattern from Machine 2

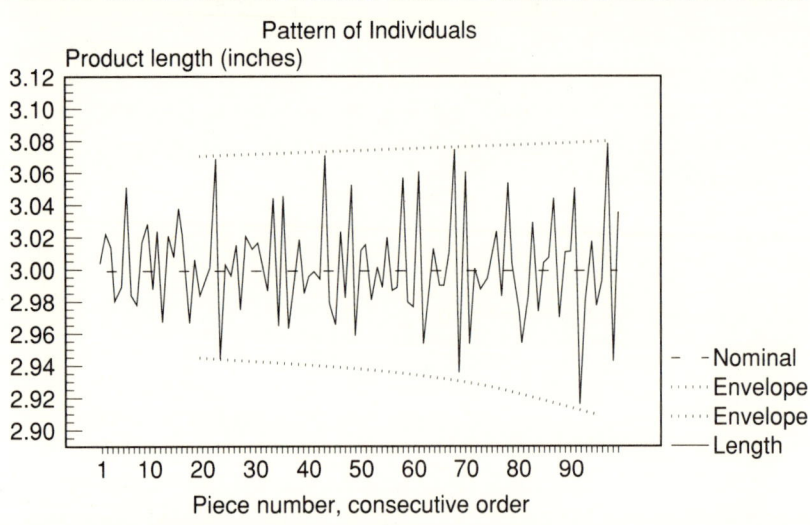

Figure 3–4 shows a plot of the data. The graph portends trouble as the process continues.

The last packet length plotted is the one after which the foil broke in the machine. Packets flapped around, the foil jammed, and the machine had to be shut down. As noted earlier, the variation increased until something had to break.

The pattern from the last 50 packets produced from Machine 2 does not indicate stability and suggests a non-normal distribution. While calculations were made of the average (3.002 inches) and the standard deviation (0.036 inch), these were only regarded as an index of the variation. The actual numerical range, as determined from the difference between the shortest and longest measurement was found to be:

Total variation = 0.160 in.

No wonder the foil broke—the variation was close to 3/16 of an inch.

**FIGURE 3–5
Sample Distribution, Machine 2**

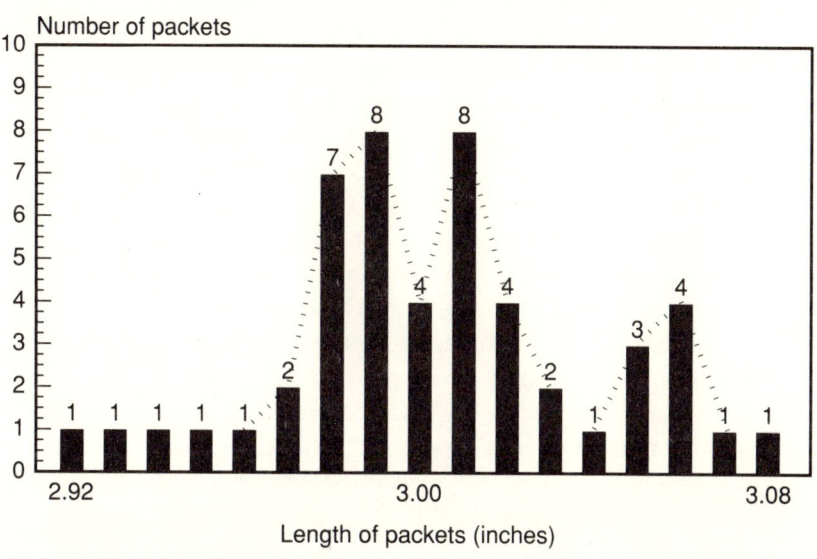

A plot of the distribution was made. This is shown in Figure 3–5. Looking at the graph, one can visualize it as a trimodal distribution (dotted envelopes), consisting of three separate causal factors that affect the total variation.

Analysis of Capability Study

The analysis revealed that neither machine was in statistical control. The basis for this observation is as follows: Neither machine exhibited a random variation of the pattern. The over-all envelope of the pattern for Machine 1 was like a wavy periodic cycle; the pattern for Machine 2 continued to expand until the foil broke and the process failed.

Since neither machine was in statistical control, there were assignable causes. *Assignable causes* means that some parts or operations in the machine were causing nonrandom variations. In electronics, that is like saying, "The variations were well above the noise level." The noise level is the level below which you can not eliminate the purely random background variation (noise) for any given system.

If the machines had been found to be in statistical control, the approach in the program would have been different. The consideration then would have been to examine the feasibility of making changes in product design and specifications, as opposed to making changes in machine design and its construction (the system of causes that produces the output).

Students in the field of statistics are cautioned about treating non-normal distributions with tools applicable only to normal distributions. With that qualification, it should be noted that using relationships for the computation of averages and standard deviations of near-normal distributions should be regarded as providing only an index of the variation relative to the particular distribution.

One other point: Why concern oneself about the length of a flimsy cleaning packet? It gets torn open, used, and the envelope is tossed away. Does it matter how long the packet is? Well, that thinking misses the point. The production system (within the existing design parameters and the existing operating conditions) was not working properly. It was producing scrap and increasing operating costs. The machine capability study showed indications that the problems could be found and rectified.

The next task was to find the specific components and/or operating conditions in the machines that were causing the variations and resultant problems.

During the course of the plant visits, Clark held meetings with Helmut and Karl to go over the concepts in statistics. The object here was to equip Helmut and Karl with the tools to check on and maintain control of the process after the machine development was completed.

To start them thinking about sources of variation in the process, Clark went over a chart with Helmut and Karl on the potential sources of variation. The chart used is shown in Figure 3–6. In effect, this was a hunting list. The next thing was to track down the gremlins.

FIGURE 3-6
Potential Sources of Variation in the System

1. Electronic and Optical Scanning System
   - Internal electronic characteristics
   - Setup and adjustment
2. General Mechanical
   - Backlash in gearing
   - Loose or worn shaft bearings
   - Worn knurled drive rollers
   - Other factors
3. Thermal Changes
   - Sealing temperature regulation
   - Variation in ambient temperature
4. Electro-Mechanical
   - Repeatability of electric clutches
   - Voltage variation and regulation
5. Raw Material Input
   - Uniformity of foil and pattern
   - Uniformity of web material
6. Machine Setup and Adjustment
   - Calibration of setup adjustments

Doug, the president, dropped into one of the meetings for a few moments after returning from a sales trip. Later he mentioned to Clark that the project was halfway through the authorized budget and he wanted to check on its progress. Clark understood the limited budget and proceeded with all haste to undertake the specific tasks necessary to bring the machines back into regulation.

The next morning Clark met with Helmut and Karl for the purpose of examining several of the machine stations in more detail. The machines had to be secured and various guards removed to be able to get at the operating components. If the machines were not shut down for major service, the production would eventually come to a halt.

One of the more significant findings was that the knurled sealing rings on Machine 2 were worn beyond useful life and needed replacing. The drive rollers also needed adjustment. Several other tooling modifications were needed. A chart on the development steps was prepared, as shown in Table 3–3.

TABLE 3-3
Machine Development Tasks

Item/Task	Object	Cost	Approved
1. Replace knurled sealing rings on Machine 2.	Improve seal and maintain tension.	$600	OK
2. Relocate sensor closer to cutoff station.	Reduce variation reaction time and scrap.	800	Defer
3. Install wider applicator guides on down run.	Prevent escape of "W"-fold moist web.	500	OK
4. Use standard eye spot on foil, black, 3/16 × 3/8.	Improve control of cutoff.	150	OK
5. Relocate applicator drive roller.	For positive control.	700	OK

The items on the list of development tasks were reviewed with Doug. As indicated in the cost and authorization column, Doug authorized work on most of the items. He wished to defer action on relocating the sensor until all other tasks were completed.

The nature of the output from each machine was now known. The associated problems and causes were identified. Helmut and Karl went on with the various development tasks.

One might ask why Clark didn't just tear the machine apart in the beginning to try to find the problem. Well, he might have done so, but there was a considerable risk of getting the machine so far out of regulation that it would have taken weeks to recover!

The capability study, while showing an out-of-control process, also indicated the potential for orderly operation well within the tolerance. And finally, as the upgrade was completed, the CleanPack Company could determine and maintain the new standards of control.

Clark provided a set of standard control charts to show the average and range of values for use in checking the process. For the reader who is not familiar with these charts, control limits are plotted to monitor the process average and range. A value that falls beyond the control limits indicates that the process needs to be checked and/or adjusted to restore normal operation.

Helmut and Karl completed work on the machine on schedule. New sealing rings were installed, along with improved tooling at several of the machine stations. The machines were serviced and thoroughly cleaned. The test runs showed that the production yield rose to a new high of 98 percent. The process was once again operating in control, and the means to maintain control were established.

In this narrative we have seen an example of what happens when a process gets out of control. The subsequent capability study shows how to go about analyzing a process so as to bring the output back into regulation. An effective quality-control program reduces the possibility of a breakdown in the process and the subsequent production losses.

CHAPTER SUMMARY

The basis for quality control lies in an *understanding* of the statistical nature of processes, and a *commitment* to support an appropriate program throughout an organization. The value of an effective program lies in an increased return on investment and profitability. The application of QC principles can be viewed as tools to this end.

The conditions for effective quality control involve many elements of a program. Following a commitment to and general understanding of the program, other elements include: provision for a broad-based program, adequate staffing and equipment, training, and responsive integration with other company functions.

The significance of the term *statistical*, as used in the field of quality control, is that the variations that occur are due to pure chance—that is, there are no assignable causes. The usefulness of knowing whether or not a process is in statistical control is that it provides information on whether or not to refine the process or reconsider the specifications of the part.

If the average value of a process and the variation (plus or minus) from the average fall within the permitted specification for the product, then the machine is capable of producing a product within the specifications.

If the values exceed the specification, then one should either adjust the machine or refine its performance to produce output to a closer distribution and/or reconsider the specification of the product. Selective assembly could also be employed, but that is usually reserved for special situations.

In using relationships in statistics, there are some implicit assumptions regarding the use of sample data. In general, applications are based upon an assumed or reasonably appropriate use of the relationships for normal bell-shaped curve data.

The general purpose of a machine capability study is to determine whether or not a machine is capable of producing output within the specification. The study can also be used as a diagnostic tool to analyze processes that have gone out of control. By comparison, the (nominal) objective of quality control is to maintain production within specification.

CHAPTER 4

MATERIAL CONTROL SYSTEMS

The narrative application in this chapter describes basic industrial engineering and management-system development work in seeking improvement in material control. The work performed in the plant with people both in the shop and management levels is described.

The chapter heading, "Material Control Systems," as used here, refers to the operating systems and procedures within a manufacturing plant, and in this case, specifically to the inventory and production control system.

The operating system of each company varies, as does the nature of its market, product line, and production system. The more significant problems that emerge may, in some cases, be traced to internal or external factors beyond the scope of control, as noted in the introductory chapter. While the details presented were about the particular situation in the plant, the type of events described are not uncommon to other organizations.

What happens in the regional, national, and global scene—and often all of a sudden—may seriously affect plant operations. In these critical situations, organizations typically embark on a development program to cope with the problem and upgrade the capabilities of the system. Sometimes the program is handled internally, while in other cases organizations utilize services to assist in the analysis and development. When services are used, management can operate with existing procedures while the work of the program goes forward, gradually implementing new developments into the system.

NARRATIVE: THE QUICK-POWER COMPANY

The pressure was beginning to build. Customers were skipping the vice president of sales to go right to the top with the question, "What's going on there? My order is two months late!" Manufacturing was also feeling the heat, and that was not the only department that was involved. The problems were, in fact, companywide. The inability to meet customer orders was only an initial symptom.

Background

The Quick-Power Company had pioneered in the development of power generators that gained a wide market acceptance. A major winter storm and the related power loss over a wide area caused a sharp increase in the demand for their product.

Problem

Prior to the extended power loss and several repeated power failures, sales had been fairly steady, but it became apparent that production could not keep up with the demand for the product. Shipping schedules were missed, excessive stockouts occurred, and the existing paperwork system was not effective in controlling production.

Management Review

A current and long-range review of the sales demand for the product line showed every indication that the sales demand would be maintained at a new high level and that regular annual increases could be expected. To respond to the change in the market, management embarked on a development program.

Program

Management interviewed and subsequently retained a consultant, following initial meetings in the plant. An initial study was authorized of the two-phase program:

Phase I: "A Preliminary Study of Inventory and Production Control Procedures."
Phase II: "Analysis and Development of Inventory and Production Control."

In the course of the initial work it was apparent to Hal, the consultant, that a strong case should be made for a broader scope in the program. The principal reasons cited were:

1. The operations of inventory and production control (alternately known and referred to as "material control") are only a part of the plant systems and procedures, and in this respect the form and content of input from other departments affect the capability and effectiveness of the function.
2. Any proposed changes to procedures within material control that affect other departments should be cleared with the associated departments.

Expressed more generally: The design and operation of a subsystem depend upon the structure, mission, and resources of the whole operation. In this case management accepted the broader scope of the project. But, it should be noted that management is often rightfully concerned (and a consultant should also be concerned) about indiscriminate expansion of a project beyond the authorized mission.

From the preliminary analysis a program was presented detailing a list of tasks to be done in the production control department and, in addition, steps that should be undertaken in the associated departments. Rather than presenting the list here, we shall go on to the actual development program as it took place.

Development Program

At the start of the project the company president, a very intelligent and capable manager, called Hal to his office. Picking up a piece of chalk, he proceeded to draw the chart on his blackboard as shown in Figure 4–1.

FIGURE 4–1
Application Chart

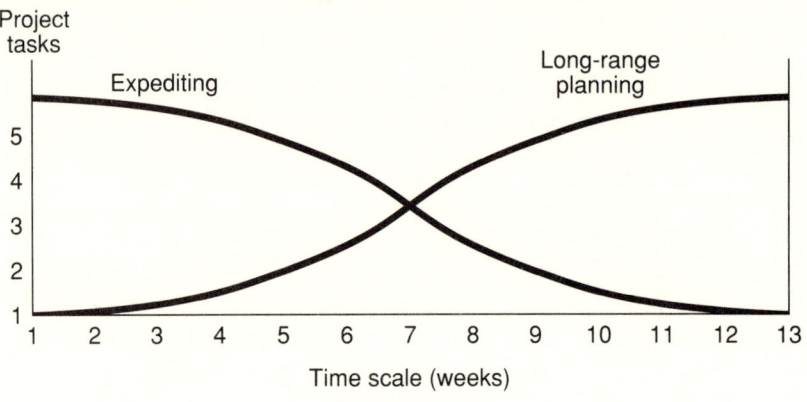

The president's "management call" was that in the immediate present, efforts were to be devoted to what he called "high-priced expediting." This was understandable. At stake was a considerable loss of business if quick action was not undertaken to fill critical customer orders. It was evident to both Hal and the president that the level of control desired would take several months to develop. Later on in the program the emphasis would shift to long-range planning.

Product Definition

Hal began his work by reviewing the stack of existing drawings and documents. What he was looking for was a manufacturing assembly chart or an indented bill of materials—a document that would reveal the structure of the product as viewed from the manufacturing standpoint. Lacking what is commonly called "manufacturing product definition," there was no way to understand how the parts of the product were assembled. Engineering had supplied a bill of materials, but it was not in a form that was useful to production control.

**FIGURE 4–2a
Product Structure Tree Chart**

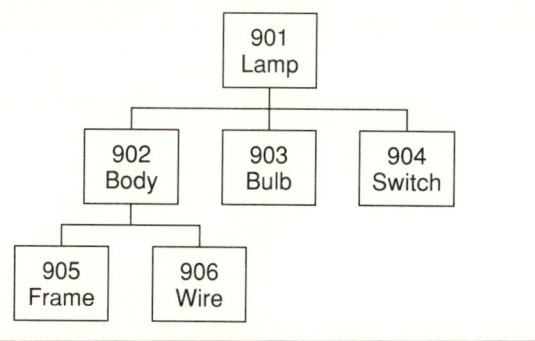

By way of background, an assembly drawing prepared by a design engineer will show relationships and/or dimensions of and between the various components, but the drawing may not show discrete physical assemblies and processes in manufacturing.

To carry this a little further, a product structure tree chart or an indented bill of materials conveys information about the structure of the product. The chart or form shows the parts and subassemblies necessary to make a given level of assembly.

As seen in Figure 4–2a and Figure 4–2b, the product structure tree and indented bill of materials illustrate the structural aspects in a form that is easy to understand. In actual practice, they may include a great deal of additional information, such as quantity requirements,

**FIGURE 4–2b
Indented Bill of Materials**

Product: 901 Lamp

Level	Part #	Description
1....	902	Body
2...	905	Frame
2...	906	Wire
1....	903	Bulb
1....	904	Switch

units of disbursements, vendors, and drawing numbers—details we will examine later.

The next step for Hal was to look at the production schedule. Sitting down with Al, the supervisor of production control, Hal noted that according to the schedule, manufacturing had accepted the commitment to produce 400 units this month. The question put to Al was, "Can 400 units be produced this month?" To this he responded, "No, but then everyone has always understood that we don't meet the schedule." With a little disbelief, but a clearer picture of the situation, Hal went on to the next subject—inventory.

A work-order ledger system was in use, but as Al stated, "Our inventory is driven by a shortage system!" In effect, work orders were written without advance knowledge of the inventory position. Production control clerks prepared work orders for parts with the necessary material requisitions. However, stores did not have a balanced inventory. This caused a frequent stock-out condition when material was requisitioned. When this happened the stock-room clerk would then prepare a request for the necessary material or purchased parts. One can visualize how open work orders accumulated as they were held up for lack of material for the work order. Hal went on to take a walk through the plant to observe other aspects of the operation.

A computer system existed in the accounting department, the use of which was understandably accounting-oriented. In a manual paperwork system, at any point in time there is an information lag or discrepancy in records between different departments. For example, an inspector may have okayed finished parts and sent them to the stockroom, but the information about the receipt of parts to the stockroom may be delayed by the amount of time it takes for accounting or production control to receive and record the information on their records. (Avoiding this can be one of the advantages of an online computer system.)

In this case, however, discrepancies in inventory were not due to the normal interdepartmental processing delays in updating transactions and inventory records. A spot check showed that quite a number of accounting records on finished parts and assemblies did not agree with the actual inventory.

Following the directives of the president, the production control order clerk, Smitty, was given the task of maintaining a critical parts list to facilitate the objective of supplying major customers. Starting from final assembly in the factory and working back to lower-level assemblies, Smitty's task was to determine where the critical shortages were. Then technical and management assistance could be given to resolve production problems such as quality, material shortages, design changes, and vendor problems. This expedient, hopefully temporary, task would ultimately be replaced by orderly material control.

By this time enough was known about the scope of the problem and both the immediate and long-range needs that it was appropriate to get the company employees together. Hal called a meeting with members of the production control department, the product engineers, the shop supervisors, and the purchasing department. The purpose was to:

- State the needs in responding to the sales demand.
- Explain the use of temporary expedient measures, which would be replaced by orderly operating systems as they were developed.
- Solicit participation in the development.

The point of the meeting was to prepare people for changes that would occur throughout the development period. Understanding the reasons for the changes would make it easier to accept new procedures as they took place.

At this point in the program several factors might be noted. Prior to the sharp rise in production demand, the existing system was working, to a point, for the "steady-state condition."

The hardest test of any system occurs when rapid changes in production levels take place. These oscillations in either direction are difficult to deal with. To compound this problem, if a major product design change is introduced at the same time, it produces a number of special demands on both management and the work force in dealing with new inventory and processes.

The reason that the organization did not immediately introduce a computer system for material control or a JIT system is that it was trying to catch up with basic planning. There is a sequence to development—product definition has to be undertaken first. After all, one cannot manufacture an ill-defined product very well.

Earlier, reference was made to the fact that a computer system existed in the accounting department. Top management realized the potential and had been considering a computer system for material control. But these major investments and system changes require a great deal of planning. To actively pursue a computer system at this time would be like attempting a casual change of a ship's rudder while it is sailing in the waters of the "Roaring Forties" east of Australia. If the conceptual operation of a system is not worked out on paper in sufficient detail, then an arbitrary computer installation will only compound the problem.

A point might be mentioned about Hal's role in this development. Throughout the consultation, Hal exercised great care to avoid usurping the functions of the supervisors and managers. Hal's role was to support and work through existing personnel. A large share of the development work performed was in the areas of manufacturing engineering and system design, functions in which the company had no qualified and designated staff at the time.

Order-Processing System

In system analysis and design work, a starting point is the system flowchart. Its purpose is to show the events that take place in sequence and the documents involved in order processing. Since a flowchart did not exist, Hal proceeded to chart the flow of documents from order entry to shipping. Because of the urgency and workload, he prepared a simplified format, as shown in Figure 4–3.

In the course of documenting the systems and procedures for an organization, it is very common to uncover

FIGURE 4–3
Simplified Chart of Existing Order-Processing System (partial illustration)

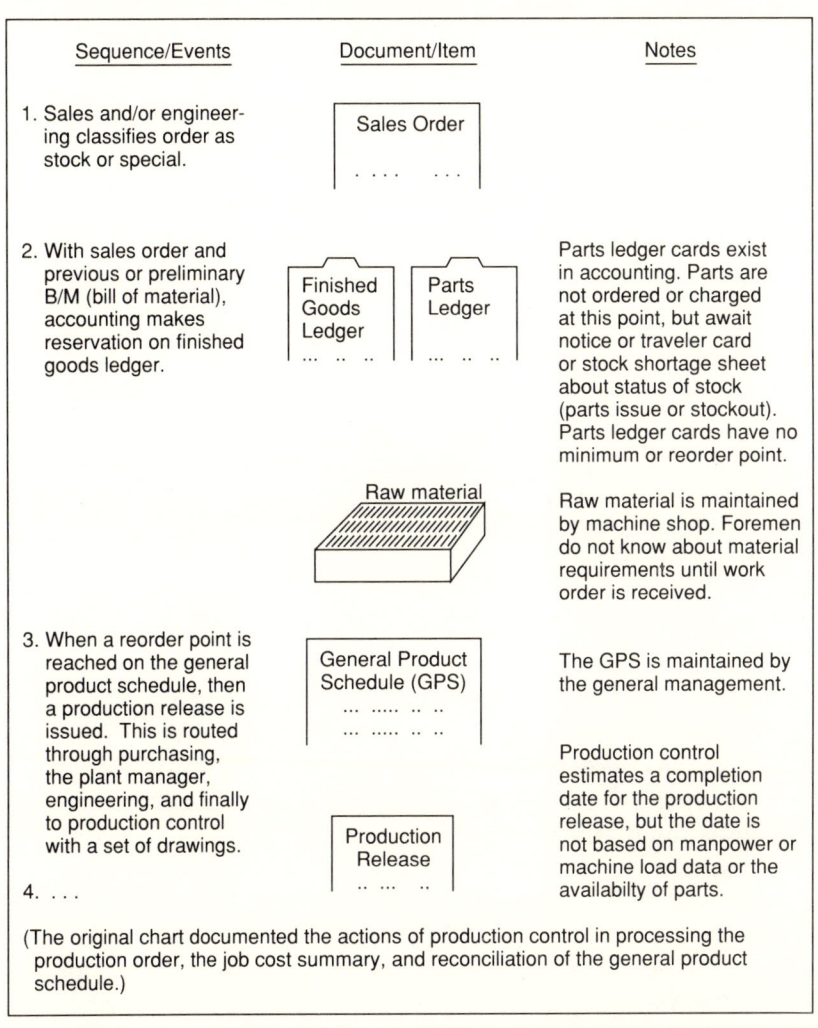

(The original chart documented the actions of production control in processing the production order, the job cost summary, and reconciliation of the general product schedule.)

unnecessary steps, open loops, or inadequate procedures. In Figure 4–3 some of the obvious flaws are indicated in the notes column. A more elaborate chart of a plant system will also show the document routing through each operating function.

Before we move on, several points about systems and procedures and their documentation are worth noting. A chart on paper does not guarantee how a system will work, certainly not forever. Nor should it. All it represents is a diagram of how a system should work under present operations. The process of preparing or updating procedures provides an opportunity to design or audit the system. In the course of subsequent events, the needs of the organization and the interactions of the line and staff persons are bound to modify the way the system works.

> While reviewing the critical parts list, it was apparent that the most serious shortage was for parts that were internally produced on a newly installed automatic screw machine. The president asked Hal to prepare an annual machine-loading computation for all parts to be produced on the new screw machine. The computation of run and setup times revealed that adequate annual capacity existed.
>
> **Machine Scheduling**
>
> The problem, however, was that there was no balanced inventory of parts "in the pipeline." In other words, a complete set of finished parts could not be issued to the assembly department for use on current work orders. To meet the critical demand, a machine schedule was prepared that specified the sequence of jobs and the quantity of parts to be run on the machine. The schedule provided for a job sequence that minimized setup changes between jobs. The schedule ultimately provided full sets of parts for product assembly.
>
> An earlier section of this chapter referred to the need for a manufacturing assembly chart. This was not for use in actual manufacturing work, but instead to derive useful production planning and control documents for work-order processing. Some of these documents will be illustrated later when the subject is pursued in more detail.
>
> At each opportunity Hal worked on a kind of "technical translation." That is, he translated engineering product-design drawings and their bills of materials to manufacturing

assemblies with bills of materials. One illustration of problems uncovered and resolved concerned the purchase and fabrication of a nylon gear for one of the products.

The product design engineer, Paul, had prepared a drawing of an injection-molded nylon gear that was to perform a certain function in the product. The nylon gear was purchased from a vendor and required a facing-off operation on a lathe in the company machine shop. The drawing, with its single part number, also showed the machined (faced-off) dimension of the part. The practice was that part numbers were to be taken as the same as the drawing numbers. As it turned out, the "finished" product, which had already been shipped, had to be recalled to replace the unmachined nylon gears!

Part-Numbering Problem

What happened? It was a common part-numbering problem! In this case Jim, the stock clerk, had only one part number under which to inventory both raw parts and finished parts. It is easy to see how a mix-up could occur. When you find the problem it is also easy to fix.

There are, of course, good ways to avoid this part-numbering problem. The measures include sound part numbering, good inventory control, and job training. As inventory and part-numbering problems were uncovered, Hal worked with Jim to explain the system. In checking back, Hal heard him say, "I like my work better now that we have a system that works."

By this time, sufficient information had been accumulated so that a more realistic projection of the production schedule could be developed. Working with Al (supervisor of production control), Hal revised and reissued the master production schedule to reflect the plant's current capability. This was very important because it enabled sales and marketing management to speak with more assurance now on commitments to customers about delivery times.

In the beginning of any project, plant people may experience some anxiety about their jobs in relation to the work of the consultant. This is understandable. *The consultant also deals with unknown aspects of the situation. One or more persons in the plant may probe for what the consultant thinks about the problem or the solution. But unfortunately there is often no single quick remedy.*

System development takes time. In this respect a consultant should exercise special care in the early stages of a project until he or she knows more about operations and establishes a good working basis with company personnel. Similarly, management should anticipate this aspect of the development process.

> In the early stages of this project the situation in the plant was tense. If a supervisor were presented with an urgently needed work order, his remark might well be, "Which hot job do you want me to stop?" After the fourth week in the program a noticeable change started to take place in the plant. A responsive can-do attitude started to emerge along with a degree of enthusiasm for the work to be done.
>
> The supervisors and work force could see changes taking place that they viewed as improvements. Workers and supervisors would come forth with problems to be resolved and suggestions to facilitate their work. They began to see more realistically events that were taking place, and they also saw that management fully supported and participated in the effort to upgrade operations.
>
> The company president was quick to order corrective measures where needed. Requirements for the approval from production control were instituted for withdrawal of parts from stores in excess of the original work order. This enabled production control to take prompt corrective actions on any impending shortages. The responsibility for ordering raw material for the machine shop was assigned to production control.
>
> Steps were taken to get the production control functions in-line on plant procedures. For example, production control was to be notified if an engineer withdrew a subassembly from production. Similarly, production control was to be notified concurrently with purchasing when purchased parts were received. Previously production control had been notified about a week after purchasing received its copy of the receiving report.

Walking through the final assembly department one morning, Hal noticed that a large blue pennant was hanging from ropes along one of the central columns in the plant, much like a masthead flag rigging on a ship. By the end of the second month, with appropriate fanfare, the flag was hoisted to the top of the column! It was an appropriate symbol of people in the plant responding to the needs and meeting the budgeted production schedule for the month.

Much remained to be done. What about staffing? Until now, adding more people would have compounded the problems. Earlier, Hal had learned that no one had performed adequate annual capacity planning for labor and equipment. Previously, new needs were handled on an individual basis.

In planning for production capacity, labor and machine-time requirements have to be determined in order to produce the various product lines in the quantities specified by an authorized production schedule. The computation will determine the staffing level and machine tool requirements in kind and quantity.

In regular meetings with foremen and production control staff it became apparent that some manpower shortages were beginning to develop and some new job classifications were needed. Pete, the foreman of the machine shop, mentioned that he could make better use of his work force on production if he had a materials handler to move parts and materials between departments.

To meet the needs in the machine shop and assembly departments, management authorized job requisitions for the growing workload in manufacturing. The quality control and production control departments also required new job classes. Hal was requested to work with supervisors to prepare job specifications for the several new classes of work. In addition he was called in to interview candidates for the new positions.

Organization

As the reader will note, very little has been said about the organization of the plant. Quite simply, the president served as the plant manager. The manager of manufacturing, the director of engineering, the vice president of sales, and the accounting, purchasing, and personnel managers all reported to the president. The supervisor of production control reported to the manager of manufacturing. Throughout the course of the development program, regular reports were prepared for the manager of manufacturing, but unfortunately, a prolonged illness precluded his direct and active participation in the program.

Sales Forecast

Clearly, the organization was undergoing considerable expansion. Hal was beginning to shift some of his attention to long-range planning. One aspect of this planning was the matter of the annual sales forecast. Hal took a walk over to the sales department. Meeting with Pat, a staff salesperson, he obtained a copy of the annual sales forecast to observe the format of the material. The data showed dollar estimates of business volume across product lines but not the quantities for the generator-system section of the business.

Capacity Planning

Hal explained to Pat, "We want to move manufacturing planning closer to customer requirements instead of manufacturing to stock." Hal went on to inquire about the possibility of obtaining estimates of the number of the system-components and replacement parts that would be required for the generator-system section of the business in future sales estimates. (This information would eventually allow the manufacturing department to compute labor and equipment requirements for the total business volume.) To the question posed, Pat's response was, "They (manufacturing) probably wouldn't know what to do with that information!" Hal recognized the "tribal" attitude, social behavior not uncommon between departments, and his only reply was, "Well, things are changing."

Production work in the plant moved along between operations, processes, and departments in batches rather than moving in a continuous process as one might see in plastic pipe extrusion or in an automated production line.

The next sections of the narrative will investigate some of the concepts of material control as relevant background to the subject.

One aspect of discrete component manufacture with characteristic batch processing is that the status of inventory at principal stages should be monitored to maintain the proper inventory levels and avoid stock shortages. A shortage that is upstream and below the required inventory level in a sequential process will work forward in the system if no corrective action is taken. In short, a stock-out will occur.

Status Report

In this program use was made of a specially prepared status report to control the production of several key parts of the product. Along with the planning basis, the report provided information on the present inventory in relation to the requirements so that corrective action could be taken when necessary.

Figure 4–4 gives an example of the format utilized to monitor fabrication of critical parts. The numerical values for operation process times have been chosen to simplify the illustration.

The report can be developed as follows:

1. List the sequence of operations and their operation process times.
2. Given the data in the illustration, note that Operation 1 (premachine frame) takes 4 hours to produce one unit.
3. The total process time for Operation 1 is simply 4 hours per unit times eight units, or 32 hours.
4. The nominal production rate for Operation 1 would be two units per day per station, that is, 8 hours divided by 4 hours per unit per station.
5. Since for Operation 1 one station can only produce two units per day, it is evident that four production stations

FIGURE 4-4
Status Report: Parts/Assemblies

Week Date: ―――/――/――
Schedule: 8 units/day
Basis: single shift 8-hour day

Product: M/G 2000
Part: main frame, fab
Part No.: M-90015
Material: main frame, cast (P-50010)

Operations	Unit Process Time (hours)	Total Process Time (hours)	Nominal Production Rate (units/day/ station)	Number of Stations	Daily Requirements from Station(s) (schedule)	Present Inventory as of (――/――/――)
1. Premachine frame	4	32	2	4	8	12
2. Prime/paint	2	16	4	2	8	4*
3. Mill face	1	8	8	1	8	8
4. Drill frame (to final assembly)	1	8	8	1	8	8
	0					

* Note: Indication of future shortage!
Action: Move and/or advance processing of 4 units from first operation to second operation; note an excess of 4 units are available.

would be necessary to meet the schedule of eight units per day (eight units divided by two units per station).
6. The total daily inventory requirements from each step in the process, whether produced by one or more similar stations to balance the flow, are eight units per day, as given in the production schedule.
7. At this point the controlling requirements are established. The next step is to determine the actual inventory at each operation or stage by a physical count or verification. In this example, note that there are only 4 units in process at operation 2 (prime/paint), while there should be 8 units to meet the schedule.

The shortage will eventually work down to final assembly unless action is taken to correct the deficiency. As indicated in this example, the action is to expedite the processing of four units (for which adequate material exists) from the first operation to the second operation.

Throughout the course of the program, Hal worked on developing the manufacturing assembly chart. For a product with over 280 parts, most of which required fabrication operations, this was a rather extensive task. The chart was finally completed during the 12th week.

Paul, the product engineer, promptly requested several copies of the assembly chart. This request may seem strange, since the assembly chart was prepared from drawings and a bill of materials supplied by the engineering department! But Hal knew that the information prepared for material control would also be useful to Paul and his draftsmen, who were trying to rectify several inadequacies and omissions in the drawings and the bill of materials.

Requests were made to Paul to supply missing part numbers from the bill of materials and to separate part numbers for finished fabricated parts as distinguished from purchased parts.

Similarly, Bill, the supervisor of cost accounting, requested copies of the document. His interest was in proper charging of material and labor costs for parts, work in process, and finished goods. His accountants could now understand the structure of the product, from raw material and purchased parts to subassemblies and the final completion of the product, without having to read an engineering drawing or trying to figure out how the product was assembled.

Manufacturing Assembly Chart

The manufacturing assembly chart was prepared in the form of a product structure tree, in this case drawn horizontally. This tree graphically portrayed the generation of component parts, fabrication, and assembly operations. The form of the initial chart is shown in Figure 4–5. The illustration here is simple enough, but the actual finished document covered a conference table!

After the chart was completed, the various operations were coded to identify machine shop operations, vendor operations, and principal inspection and test operations. The next step was to prepare a set of convenient breakdowns that classified and organized the data that material control needed.

The set of prepared documents included:

1. Parts made from raw material (stock requirements).
2. Parts with second-operation work (purchased parts requiring fabrication).
3. Purchased parts used "as is."
4. Indented bill of materials for machine shop assemblies.
5. Stock issue for final assembly.

Indented Bill of Materials

An illustration of a detailed indented bill of materials is shown in Figure 4–6. The generation of assemblies and parts and the sources of their raw materials are shown in the column headed "Level." In a more comprehensive indented product structure the components may extend to nine or more levels.

Having information in this form was very useful. Anyone who needed to know what parts were necessary for

FIGURE 4–5
Form of the Manufacturing Assembly Chart

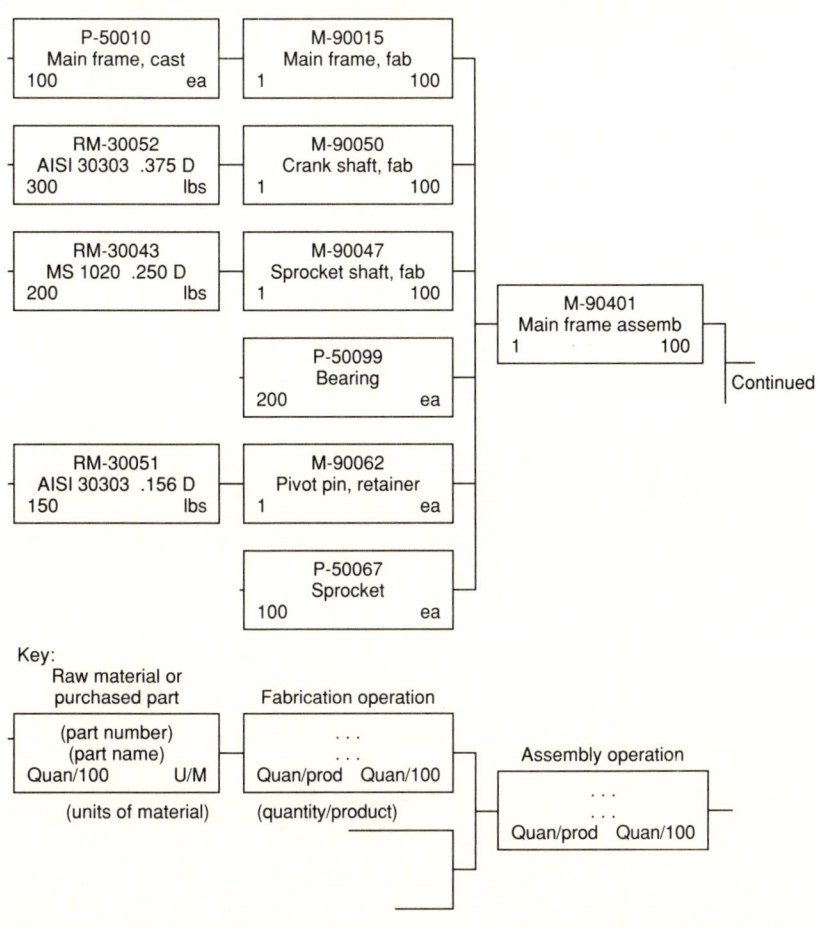

an assembly could readily find out from the hard-copy documentation. Information on material requirements was similarly available. New employees in production control could be introduced to their tasks with documents that were understandable and useful in preparing work orders and checking on material requirements.

As Hal walked through the plant on one of his regular tours, he reflected on the status of the program. While the

FIGURE 4–6
Indented Bill of Materials Showing Generation of Assembly

Assembly	Level	Part #	Description	DWG	Vendor	U/M	Qty
M90401		M90401	Main frame assembly	90050		ea.	1
	1	M90015	Main frame, fab	90051		ea.	1
	2	P50010	Main frame, cast	90052	C42	ea.	1
	1	M90050	Crank shaft, fab	90053		ea.	1
	2	RM30052	AISI 30303, .375D	RM30052	R16	lbs.	3
	1	M90047	Sprocket shaft, fab	90063		ea.	1
	2	RM30043	MS 1020, .250D	RM30043	R16	lbs.	2
	1	P50099	Bearing	RM50099	M27	ea.	2
	1	M90062	Pivot pin, retainer	90078		ea.	1
	2	RM30051	AISI 30303, .156D	RM30051	R16	lbs.	1.5
	1	P50067	Sprocket	90037	M27	ea.	1

production rate recovered to meet the demand, he knew that he had accomplished only the basic manufacturing documentation and planning. It was time to move on to a higher level of production and material control system. This would be the introduction of the JIT "pull system" for fabrication of parts and computerized scheduling of final assembly.

An extensive search led to the appointment of a new manager of manufacturing. In addition the company hired a manufacturing engineer for the new position created. In contrast to the earlier excitement and pressures during the project, operations at the plant were approaching an even pace.

The production control department had a work order record system. To complement and support this system the department installed an interim ledger record system for raw material, parts, and finished goods. This record system was tied in with the accounting system. Production control could now readily obtain information on the status of any part. The ledger record showed receipts, issues, materials on order, and the balance of the stock.

An SPI (standard procedure instruction) was prepared which detailed the complete system. The SPI described the actions to be taken and identified the responsible departments in the processing of work orders.

So far there has been no discussion of personnel qualifications. If asked about personnel, Hal would provide his appraisal. However, the only reason to broach the subject of personnel would have been to obstruct the program, which did not occur. The mission of the development program was to upgrade the material control system. The new manager of manufacturing undertook the further development of the system with his staff.

In the beginning of this chapter, the statement was made that the problem was companywide. At this point we have seen that departments other than production control contributed to the overall problems in the plant. Engineering had not really defined the product. Sales had not supplied complete information in a form that was useful for production planning across all product lines. Other factors, along with changes in design, greatly added to the manufacturing workload.

In summary, what had the program accomplished?

- It had upgraded material control and put production back on schedule.
- It had developed manufacturing bills of materials as an essential part of material control.
- It had improved operating morale, and personnel in the plant were contributing to further developments.
- It had established annual manufacturing capacity planning.
- It had initiated the selection of a computer-based material control program and the introduction of JIT as the next phase of the development.

Before leaving the subject of material control, we will discuss briefly some of the approaches to this subject that have gained considerable attention. These approaches and concepts are part of an interrelated spectrum of programs in manufacturing planning and quality control.

MATERIAL CONTROL IN TRANSITION

Material control systems have been undergoing extensive changes. Competition and the potential for reducing production costs have caused manufacturers to improve their systems. Traditional departmental functions have yielded to larger considerations. The scope of the concept has expanded to include the full cycle, from the supplier of the material to the customer. In companies where these systems have been installed, workflow and manufacturing planning have focused on straight-through processes, with little or no inventory between each process. Total-system concepts are emerging.

Just in Time

One of the concepts mentioned in chapter 1 is "just in time" (JIT),[1] also called "stockless production."[2] This system seeks to provide and process the required material at the time necessary to meet customer requirements. When successfully employed, JIT reduces inventory carrying costs, provides for quick detection of defects, and reduces plant space requirements.

Manufacturing Cells and Total Quality Control

There are several related concepts, including manufacturing (work) cells,[3] with short setup capabilities. The installation of a "total quality control" (TQC)[4] program is considered essential for proper functioning of these new systems. In a study by Jef Barrett, an installation of JIT and TQC produced a 60-percent decrease in average inventory, a 67-percent decrease in scrap, and a manufacturing-cycle time reduction from 12 weeks to 4 weeks.[5]

Flexible Manufacturing Systems

Flexible Manufacturing Systems (FMS)[6] feature NC machine tools, a materials-handling system, cutting tools, work-holding devices, and a computer control network.

The reduction of inventory levels has several direct and indirect benefits. However, in periods of short material supply or rapidly changing prices, companies may wish to modify their inventory policy to avoid stock-outs and to respond to major changes in material cost.

MRP and Capacity-Driven Systems

Computerized material control systems for manufacturing can be classified in two major categories. One features make-to-stock, lead-time scheduling as in MRP. The other scheme features real-time, job-based *capacity-driven systems,* as in ProfitKey[7] software. In linked cellular manufacturing systems, only final assembly is scheduled. The kanban (card/container) system signifies work and parts requirements.

In the make-to-order, job-based, capacity-driven system, the production schedule is based upon actual loads and capacities in the work centers. This system is generally more suitable for job shops and custom manufacturing.

In an MRP system, the capacity of the work center is taken into account in the original planning base, but fixed lead-time computations are utilized in the production scheduling based upon authorized stock levels. This system is more common for standard design high-volume production.

It is evident that care should be exercised in the selection of a computer program to determine that it provides a suitable kind and level of control for the specific application.

CHAPTER SUMMARY

The material control system of a company may vary as does the nature of its market, product line, and production. It is important to employ and develop a material control system that is appropriate for the characteristics and needs of the organization.

It is essential to perform the "technical translation" of engineering product design and assembly layouts to the form required by material control personnel. A common format is the indented parts list, showing the parts and subassemblies required for a given assembly. The document should also show the drawing number, vendor, units of material, and quantity requirements per assembly.

In the analysis and development of a material control system, if the order-processing system is not documented, it should be charted to reveal possible inadequacies or open loops in the system. The audit alone is often helpful in upgrading the system.

Regardless of the material control system, manufacturing-capacity planning for labor and capital equipment requirements should be performed.

If an effective JIT-kanban (bin/card) reorder system is not employed in a discrete component manufacturing system with characteristic batch processing, the status of inventory at principal stages should be monitored to maintain the proper inventory levels and avoid stock shortages. A shortage that is upstream and below the required inventory level in a sequential process will work forward in the system if no corrective action is taken.

As is apparent, the systems and techniques employed in material control are undergoing considerable transition. The more noteworthy system, JIT (Just In Time), when successfully employed, reduces inventory carrying costs, provides for quick detection of defects, and reduces plant space requirements.

Other concepts that tie in with JIT are cellular manufacturing, setup time reduction, preventive maintenance, and TQC (Total Quality Control).

Computerized material control systems for manufacturing can be classified in two major categories. One features make-to-stock, lead-time scheduling as in MRP. The other scheme features real-time, job-based capacity-driven systems as in ProfitKey software.

In the make-to-order, job-based capacity-driven system, the production schedule is based upon actual loads and capacities in the work centers. This system is generally more suitable for job shops and custom manufacturing.

In an MRP system, the capacity of the work center is taken into account in the original planning base, but fixed lead-time computations are utilized in the production scheduling based on authorized stock levels. This system is more common for standard design high-volume production.

It is evident that care should be exercised in the selection of a computer program to determine that it provides a suitable kind and level of control for the specific application.

CHAPTER 5

FACILITIES AND LAYOUT

The kind of manufacturing facilities available and the manner in which parts and assemblies move from one work station to another in a manufacturing process have an effect on the options and capabilities of production systems. More specifically, increases in productivity and improvements in quality are affected by the kind and layout of facilities. Further, the provision for first-rate facilities and layout complement the productive manufacturing technologies and systems cited in earlier chapters.

Gradual changes in product design or the introduction of major new product lines, along with changes in manufacturing technology, ultimately cause plant layouts to become obsolete. This is why a master workflow plan for a plant and the associated layout of supporting facilities and services require periodic upgrading and/or major new planning over periods of time.

Major plant expansion and development programs are given a considerable amount of attention by top management. This is understandable. Large investments are required in new buildings and equipment. Executives who understand the need for providing for economic production and long-range capability aggressively pursue investment in the capital facilities. They realize that equipment and buildings get "used up." One of the ways they maintain a competitive edge and provide for new business opportunities is to reinvest in productive facilities and an efficient plant layout.

NARRATIVE: SOUTHERN/BELL FURNITURE COMPANY

The tall, distinguished man crossed the town square of the historic southern city. He was on a delicate mission. As vice president of manufacturing for the Southern/Bell Furniture Company, Edward was exploring the possibility of acquiring a parcel of land from a prominent local lady recently widowed. The property was adjacent to the principal manufacturing site of Southern/Bell. Use of the land was vital to long-range expansion of the facility. The meeting went well.

Edward mentioned, "If Southern/Bell acquired the property, part of the land would be used to provide a small park with a suitable dedication. Further, if expansion of the manufacturing facility took place, it would provide new jobs for local people." The gracious lady smiled and stated that she would be glad to make the land available. Edward went on to express his appreciation. They both agreed that the lawyers could take it from there.

Returning to the plant, Edward felt pleased. Negotiating for a property was certainly not in his job description, but if that was what it took to provide for the long-range planning and development of the manufacturing facility—he was on it, always ahead! He invested his time in things that mattered. At the same time, details about production tooling in the plant or about personnel matters did not escape him. In a word, he was a competent and effective executive—well liked and respected. So much so that people in the plant thought of him as "the company."

Over the past nine years, Ed, as he was known in the plant, had been involved in several modifications to existing buildings in order to accommodate new equipment required to meet customer sales. But he knew that time was running out. To maintain leadership in both volume and product line, the company needed to undertake design and construction of a major new building that would provide for an integrated manufacturing facility at their main site, located on River Road. A whole new concept in workflow and layout would be required along with some new production facilities and utilities. In brief, Ed felt a development program was necessary to provide for higher productivity and to meet the capacity for the projected market.

Several months earlier, Ed had opened a meeting with Roger, the director of engineering, by saying, "We need to prepare a master plan for an integrated facility here at River Road. The Grove Street operation has become ineffective and costly, and we don't have adequate long-range capacity here at River Road."

Roger responded, "Apparently we can more actively pursue the building proposal. Good! I have just been reviewing the accounts for building repair and equipment maintenance. The records show substantial increases in recent years. A share of these charges would not be required if we could undertake a major facilities development program. We could devote more time to the product and new production tooling on which we have a growing backlog of work."

"Yes, I know, Roger," Ed replied. "That, among other reasons, is why we have to make a strong case for a major new facility development program. We have to focus on the products, production, and customer needs and not on holding our buildings together and trucking parts all over the place.

"We will talk more about the plans for the facility. I would like to see some concepts and a preliminary schedule. Would you initiate contact with our industrial architect and two builders as a preliminary step until we determine how we are going to proceed on this? Give them a plant tour, and inquire about their interest. Ask them about the current nominal cost per square foot for industrial building space of the type we have in the west-end fab building. When we have enough preliminary information and final approval, we can schedule a general meeting on the program. And—oh, charge any time to a special-projects account. Ask Hanna in accounting for a charge number."

Subsequently Roger obtained unit cost estimates on building construction along with other data on utilities that would be required. He also asked Greg, his industrial engineer, to check all building shell drawings to be sure they were updated to include any modifications to existing buildings. Similarly, engineering was to check the site drawings to be sure they were up to date showing the property lines, utility notations, and any easements. Roger also passed on the information that, while acquisition of the adjacent property they were seeking was not yet finalized, indications were that it would be obtained. And finally he asked Greg, "Would you prepare a report with some economic data on our plant layout and site situation and then go on to sketch some general layout concepts for the consolidation and integration of facilities here at our River Road site?"

While he knew it was a challenging assignment, Greg responded with an enthusiastic, "Yes. I have been thinking about how we could eliminate the excess materials handling we have, both within and between the plants. This might also give us a chance to replace some of the obsolete equipment in the plants. What's the time schedule on this?"

Roger responded, "Well, Ed wants us to move along on this. My feeling is we should complete the preliminary planning within several weeks. The expansion proposal will be presented at the corporate management meeting in two months."

KINDS OF LAYOUTS

In the early stages of planning a new plant layout or revising an existing layout, considerable information and data need to be prepared. But first, we will discuss the different kinds of layouts.

One of the fairly general approaches is the layout of facilities according to the *product fabrication/assembly sequence*. This approach, coupled with two complementary procedures, can be very effective. The procedures include scheduling production to customer orders and ordering materials for delivery only when needed and in the quantities needed.

Both the layout and procedural aspects provide for:

- Reduced plant space requirements.
- Lower inventory cost.
- Quick reaction to quality problems.

The product assembly sequence, however, is only one of four concepts in layout planning. In some cases the assembly sequence is of minor importance. The handling between operations may be of insignificant value or size, or the specifics of the material delivery system may determine the use of other concepts. A *functional (process) grouping of facilities by machine type* is employed where the desire is to obtain the advantages of multiple machine assignment, efficient layout, and uniformity of the material delivery system. An example of this is the grouping of automatic screw machines in a single work center.

A third concept is to provide for complete *construction and assembly of a product at a single location*. The construction and assembly of a logging mill constitute an example of a product that may be fabricated at a single location.

The fourth and newest approach consists of *work-cell manufacturing layout, employing group technology*. In this system, the group technology analysis identifies families of parts that can be produced in a work cell consisting of several machines serviced by one or more operators. Ultimately, each manufacturing cell is then arranged according to the general production manufacturing sequence. Most layouts evolve from some combination of the concepts, depending on the specific product and process factors.

There is a major difference between developing a plant layout and the building design for a totally new site, and replanning the layout of an existing facility. In totally new layout planning at a new site, there are few building constraints except for topographical features and code and zoning regulations. The manufacturing requirements and workflow can determine the configuration and features of the building. In relayout and/or expansion of an existing building, attempts are made to utilize the existing structure and still retain much of the value of a good workflow.

All plans, of course, have to include provision for personnel and supervisory requirements, supporting services, utilities, material and inventory needs, security and safety features, and provision for processes that require a "clean room," isolation, or any other special considerations.

> Greg was the kind of a guy who could think well with a pencil in hand. As he undertook the assignment he started to jot down notes in outline form:
>
> ### Analysis Layout/Site Situation— Consolidation/Integration
> 1. Grove Street site: age of building complex 49 years, facilities and layout limit effective manufacturing and incur high maintenance cost.
> 2. Two-site situation: trucking costs between plants, parts damage in transit, reduced quality control of sequential process.
> 3. River Road site: good concrete/steel building, exceeding production capacity, manufacturing cost increases due to some equipment and plant space problems.
>
> Reaching into one of his desk drawers, he withdrew the town map. Selecting the proper section, he made a photocopy showing the location of Southern/Bell's two sites in the town. Greg also made a miniaturized copy of the building shell drawing of the River Road facility and the other building across town at the Grove Street site. In order to portray the building and site situation, he assembled a composite drawing as shown in Figure 5–1.
>
> In the subsequent days, Greg tactfully pursued discussions with manufacturing supervisors and managers. They reviewed the background on the building and workflow problems. Data were gradually accumulated from the personnel department records and other sources in the engineering office.

**FIGURE 5–1
Site/Layout Features**

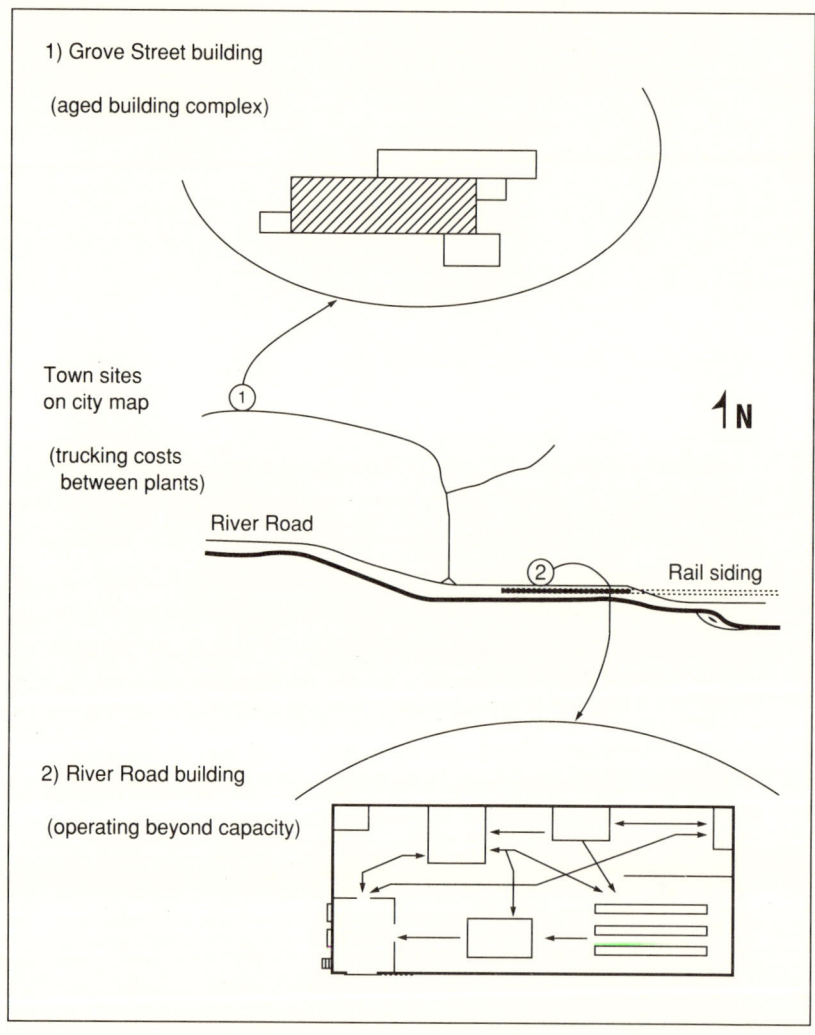

Greg decided to prepare a comprehensive report that could be passed up the line and to accounting and sales executives who were not as familiar as he with the details.

The thinking here was that after their review, they would be in a better position to understand the manufacturing situation. Greg's report went as follows:

Plant Consolidation/Integration at River Road

Background on Workflow

Rough planed lumber (maple and oak) in 4 × 4, 6 × 4, and 8 × 4 sizes is delivered to the factory in bundles from which batch lots are withdrawn for processing. The process starts with checking the stock for defects (which are removed), after which the lot order is finished planed. The planed stock is placed on a skid and moved by a hand-operated or powered truck to the next operation. In the subsequent operations, the order is rip/sawn to size, after which it is processed through the molder, tenoner, and/or drilling machines. The parts are assembled with clamping fixtures, glue, screw fasteners, and other hardware. This is a somewhat simplified description of the fabrication process, as work may recycle back and forth between work centers, repeating or skipping some operations.

In most cases the stock moves from skid to operation to skid within the machine group. This provides for an efficient cycle at the machine station. When the next machine tool in the process is not immediately adjacent, the stock is trucked to that next operation. The parts are then assembled. After final sanding, staining, and sealing, the assemblies are moved to a staging and loading area for the lacquer and bake cycle. For this process, assemblies and parts are placed in fixtures on a conveyer for processing through the lacquer and bake cycle. After final rubbing and inspection, the product is packed for shipping to our distribution centers.

Sizable quantities of work in process may exist in various stages of fabrication throughout the process. This occurs for several reasons. As noted earlier, different operations have different production rates. They vary from a low of a five-second cycle for some drilling operations to rates of 12 minutes for other operations. The conveyerized lacquer process runs at a fixed rate. Parts on skids are accumulated for loading on the conveyer where the lacquer/bake cycle is started. For a good color match between related parts they must be loaded in close proximity rather than a random order. In addition, some priority job lots take precedence over previously scheduled work which is then set aside for the rush job.

For the reasons mentioned, temporary storage areas are provided for work in process. The configuration of the product varies, as does the process. Complete automated processing is not employed, except for the lacquer/bake cycle. Process factors, such as the risk of contamination and pick-up of dirt, also make it desirable to isolate some operations, like separation of sanding from lacquering.

Context of Manufacture

The River Road plant (now operating on three shifts) has, for some time, been experiencing congestion, interference, and delays between work centers. The accumulation of work in process between the woodworking and lacquer department areas is, in part, planned; but it also occurs between some woodworking operations. Work piles up on skids and trucks, extending over into aisles, impeding efficient materials handling as well as contributing to potentially hazardous situations.

Considering the nature of the product—furniture—its value consists of aesthetic qualities and appearance as well as the functional properties. The product can lose its value because of a nick, scratch, or speck of dirt. The probability of these losses increases without adequate space for controlled movement of work in process and balancing of production capacities between machine tools and the work centers. An additional molder is required to balance the workflow and an obsolete planer should be replaced. Production scheduling and control is also a factor here, and the department is working on the scheduling problem.

Because of space limitations, some of the parts at River Road are sent by truck to Grove Street for a special silk screen and printing operation. The parts are then returned to River Road for the final lacquer overcoat. Turned work on a profile lathe is also performed at Grove Street and returned to River Road. The use of two separate plants causes an interruption of sequential production processes as well as the divided control and management of the operations. The cost of the associated interplant materials handling is only a segment of the growing and otherwise hidden operating costs.

Even with inspection and quality control, defects in the process may not be apparent until all components are assembled at River Road. Damage to a part may occur after inspection and in transit between plants. Some damaged parts can be salvaged by stripping and rework, but this increases production costs. The above-cited losses and extra costs are not chargeable to ordinary operator errors or failure in supervision; rather they fall beyond the normal expectation because of space limitations, several equipment needs, and divided facilities.

(The report went on to detail the pilot upholstered furniture process that was set up at Grove Street, but the details are not presented here. Instead, the account moves on to Greg's writeup on plant capacity.)

Index of Plant Capacity

A numerical index can be presented to show the current operating level in relation to the normal (planned) capacity staffing level of the River Road facility. Normal capacity staffing, in this case, is defined as the economic operating level in the use (and availability) of labor and facilities for a given production rate and specific layout. Table 5–1 shows the normal and the current levels at the River Road plant. The percentage increase over normal level is also shown. Operating above (or below) the normal staffing level causes variances in labor and facilities usages.

From the table it can be seen that the operation is running in excess of the normal (planned) level. The difference between the first and second shift is, in part, intentional (for supervisory reasons), and also because of less service people on the second shift. The third shift, of course, is only marginal

TABLE 5-1
Operating Level, River Road Site

	Shifts			
Staffing*	1	2	3	Total
Normal staffing	125	70	10	205
Current staffing	147	87	12	246
Percent above planned level	18	24	20	20

* Entries represent direct labor and maintenance staffing.

and lacks the resources of the service and maintenance functions.

In general, increasing production beyond the current level is limited by space and machine capacity. Operating beyond peak capacity increases unit production costs. There are several reasons for this. Access time for regular machine maintenance and repair tends to be reduced. This in turn increases unscheduled down time, with the associated production losses in addition to accumulation of idle time during repair or trouble shooting.

If the production demand increases 10 percent per year, as it did last year, then we will have nearly reached the maximum plant capacity of present facilities. Improvements in our manufacturing technology will provide some additional capacity, but even more automated processes take large amounts of space.

Management has used some special methods to deal with the current operating problems. The creation of an operator's pool at River Road performs some assembly work when machine troubles or capacity problems occur. The overemployment of operators for the River Road facility (because of absenteeism) is a method of meeting production demands with present facilities. The hot ambient air temperature in the lacquer room, along with other factors, is felt to have a bearing on operator absenteeism.

We have already seen the background and basis for the plant expansion and integration of facilities at River Road. The following section examines projected savings that can be recovered through a plant development program.

TABLE 5–2
Basic Savings from Development Program

Direct and indirect labor savings:	$232,700
Manufacturing control and labor effectiveness	
Elimination of duplicate positions in plants	
Improved productivity from air treatment	
Reduction of maintenance (single location)	
Material saving:	8,500
Parts damage in trucking	
Machines, equipment, tools:	24,000
Improved tool control	
Disposal of obsolete and surplus machines	
Building utilities, services, and insurance:	38,100
Heating costs at Grove Street plant	
Electric power costs, lower KW rating	
Insurance	
Plant security:	5,000
ADT costs at Grove Street plant	
Interplant trucking and personal travel:	37,100
Total	$345,400

Economic Factors

This section presents the economic aspects of the proposed plant development. In this analysis, the cost figures used are based on actual records where available—otherwise the best estimates are given. The objective is to convey the basic economic factors and their order of magnitude as an indication of the need and merit of the proposed major building program. The analysis determines the recoverable operating costs that may be realized through the combination of a plant expansion at River Road, disposal of the Grove Street site, and the consolidation of all operations at River Road.

    A detailed analysis of the projected basic savings and cost data has been prepared in engineering. The entries for each category of labor, material, and other costs listed in the worksheet are based upon the specific factors that apply at each of the two sites and the associated trucking between each of them. From this worksheet, Table 5–2 and Table 5–3 have been prepared. While the potential savings are significant, they should be regarded as gross (not net)

TABLE 5-3
Cost and Economic Data, Building/Consolidation Program

Cost of 70,000 sq. ft. building extension at River Road:	$2,100,000
The additional plant space requirement is based upon consolidation of manufacturing operations at the River Road site.	
The cost of the new plant expansion is based upon a rate of $30 per sq. ft.	
The additional space should be adequate for 3–5 years at a sales increase of 10 percent per year.	
Life of building extension:	40–45 years
Acquisition of land at River Road site:	
Acquisition of a parcel of land at River Road site is under active negotiations.	
An option on additional parcels should be considered if subsequent long range expansion at this site is planned.	
Market value of Grove Street land and building:	$300,000
Annual building depreciation charge is at $17,800.	
Cost of moving operations, (Grove Street to River Road):	$200,000
Increase in taxes on River Road buildings:	$35,000
Higher capitalized value of buildings.	

savings—as this analysis does not account for the share of capital building costs required to produce at the current level. The next step in a subsequent report would be to compare the present manufacturing cost at the present production rate with the manufacturing cost in a consolidated facility. Unit cost could also be shown at increased production rates that would account for the economies of scale, up to the new higher plant capacity.

In summary, up to this point, the two prime factors are:

1. Providing for present and future capacity.
2. Providing for manufacturing productivity.

In approaching layout planning, instead of plunging into details, it is important to devote a considerable amount of thought and work to developing general concepts and layout plans. At this stage, an opportunity exists to introduce new concepts and improvements over current layouts and operations. In the plans, provision should also be made for a next-stage expansion if that is anticipated at the site.

General Approach in Layout

There is an organized approach that attempts to minimize materials handling between successive operations or work centers. The approach can be applied to either a composite (micro) product assembly process or a (macro) grouping of work centers by function. The general approach is as follows:

1. *Flow of materials. Determine the sequence in the movement of materials between operations and/or work centers.*
2. *Activity relationships. Obtain a set of the indices of the (cost-related) volume of material movement between operations or work centers. (This travel chart can be prepared much like a chart on a common road map. The entries would consist of a quantitative index of the cost of materials handling between each position or work center.)*
3. *Operation/work center size requirements. Compute the physical space requirements for operations/work centers.*
4. *Relative location of operation/work centers. Arrange operation/work centers in relation to each other with regard to their size and relational importance—all within some acceptable configuration or actual building space.*
5. *General layout scheme. The previous steps will have provided one or more alternate layout schemes from an idealized mathematical approach. One or more of these general layout schemes can then be used to seek agreement on a general layout. The drawing may also show the workflow, main aisles, and other features not expressly treated in the analysis. The purpose at this stage is to assure understanding of the general plan, evaluate its merits, and ultimately obtain agreement on the general plan.*
6. *Detailed layout plan. Following acceptance of the general layout, the detailed layout of each work center and operation can be*

prepared and reviewed for subsequent approval. Approval should start from the bottom up (line supervisors to general management).

There are several computer programs[1] that may aid in working through the analysis. Each of the programs has an array of different features. The analysis of workflow and materials handling is, however, only one of the many considerations, as was mentioned earlier.

Greg's report continued as follows:

Preliminary Layout/Building Considerations
While the building specifications will be prepared in future weeks, the following preliminary layout considerations will serve as a guide to planning the new building:

1. The new building should be positioned in line as an easterly extension of the existing building. This will provide for installation of the new master layout plan without affecting present production.
2. The bay and column spacing should align with those in the present building.
3. Utilities in new construction should provide for air treatment and conditioning. Plans should also be developed to reduce the excess heat load at the lacquer and bake cycle in the existing building. Additional air make-up is required.
4. Provision should be made for increased unit dust collection at each woodworking machine.
5. Truck docks and a rail siding access door will be required.
6. Provision should be made for improved chemical waste treatment.
7. Consideration should be given to planning a lunch/snack room.

Layout Concept
The layout concept provides for an in-line workflow from the east end of the proposed new building extension through to the west end of the present building on River Road. Incoming

rough-planed lumber arriving by rail or truck would be processed through finish plane. The material would then move to the woodworking area to be processed in the new work cells. Finished parts then would move to a new conveyorized assembly line. The assembly line would consist of a combination of controllable live and dead conveyors at the proper height for product assembly. The general layout concept is shown in Figure 5–2. The conveyor from assembly would be tied into the lacquer and bake conveyor in the existing building. An alternate concept, of course, would be just to fit the operations from the Grove Street plant into the new space, but this would only provide a marginal advantage over existing operations.

Schedule

A preliminary schedule for the project is presented in Figure 5–3. At this stage it merely lists some of the major phases of the project.

This ended Greg's report on the project. During the preparation of the report, as mentioned earlier, Greg frequently checked with manufacturing supervisors and managers on various details. In particular, he discussed the concept of a conveyorized assembly line with Matt, the production manager. Greg also mentioned the use of leveling units for heavy stock that would position pieces at waist height for the operator. Matt stated, "I like the idea of our operators not having to lift the parts—we get a lot of backstrain problems. But we would have to be careful in setting up the process so our people could adjust to a new conveyorized method."

At that point Greg responded, "Yes, you're right. To help in acceptance, perhaps your people could be involved in the development. There are other aspects. To balance the workflow, the work content at each station would change. Maybe qualified operators who wished to could go on to other work stations. This would provide for more flexibility."

Ultimately Greg's report was reviewed by his boss, Roger. With some editing and the addition of more detailed

FIGURE 5-2
General Layout Concept

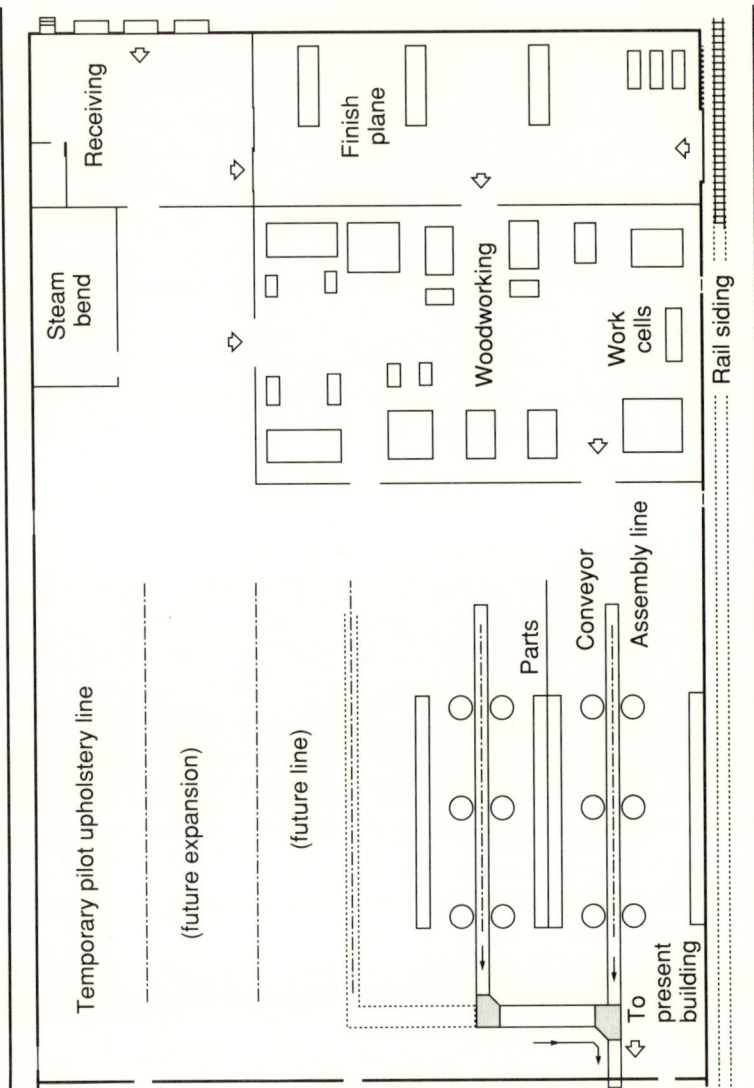

FIGURE 5–3
Project Schedule

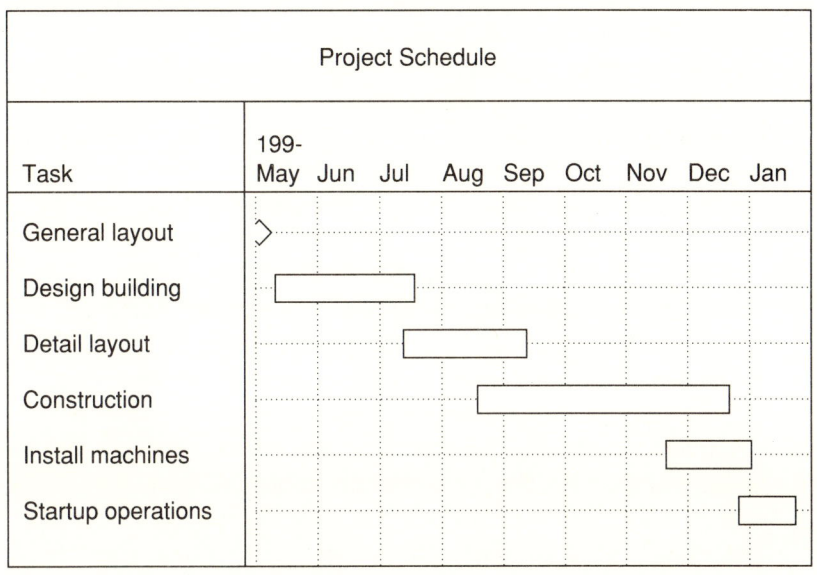

cost data the report was passed up to Ed, the vice president of manufacturing.

Ed was in the middle of preparing his own proposal for the program to be presented to the Board of Directors. Stopping to read the engineering report was a welcome break in his work. He found several useful concepts and some of the data he needed for the proposal.

In time, the proposal was completed. It was a thorough presentation—a strong case for the development program. Starting with an executive summary, the proposal continued with a detailed market evaluation, and in order, a section on manufacturing, engineering, and layout concepts and plans.

The executive summary opened with, "The Southern/Bell plant integration and expansion program will be necessary to meet projected sales forecasts during the coming years." The summary went on to list the principal features of the expansion progam including: provision for increased

102 Chapter 5

capacity, improved productivity in operations, and expanded product design and manufacturing engineering. The strategic factors were mentioned and subsequently detailed in the body of the proposal. The engineering section of the proposal listed every phase and task in the project, including building, initial preparation, new utilities, equipment relocation, site work, and additional equipment. The estimates were further broken down by expense and/or capital cost for each category. The detailed section further classified the cost as material or labor.

By now, almost everybody knew about the building proposal. They were all thinking about how it might affect their jobs. Their feelings, however, were positive. Even the pace of work in the office and in the factory seemed to pick up.

The day of the board meeting finally arrived. There were no cheers that anyone could hear from the boardroom, but as Ed and the members of the group left the paneled room, you could see quiet smiles of assurance. The program—ultimately $3 million—was authorized!

The treasurer of Southern/Bell wasn't entirely pleased. He wanted the $3 million to buy another company, but investing in their own manufacturing technology won out.

It wasn't long after the meeting that the new parcel of land on River Road was acquired. Ed thought it was about time to get the group together in a project meeting on the program. He called a meeting to be held in the factory conference room with the engineering staff and manufacturing supervisors and managers.

The people started to arrive at the appointed time, 10 o'clock. Grabbing a chair, the head of quality control wiped a thin layer of dust off of the seat. Ed entered with his production manager, Matt, and Roger, and Greg from engineering. Considering the occasion, the social talk was fairly upbeat.

Ed started the meeting, stating, "The purpose of this meeting is to come to agreement on a general layout plan for the new building. Greg has worked up a concept."

Turning to Greg, Ed asked, "Why don't you proceed?"

Stepping up to the table, Greg spread an enlarged drawing of the concept, similar to the drawing shown earlier in Figure 5–2. Greg was about to proceed when a plant supervisor walked in swinging his previously injured arm, now entirely healed but still in a cast. As the supervisor sat down, dropping his heavy cast on the table, some of the plaster chips shattered over the plans. At that point Greg said, "Well, while it wasn't a bottle, I guess we can say the plans have been christened!" Everyone roared.

After the laughter subsided, Greg presented the features of the general layout concept. During the course of the presentation there were some questions.

One of the production supervisors asked, "How will the legs of a table slide over the roller conveyor?"

To that, Greg answered, "We will have light-weight recyclable flat forms, counterbored to hold the legs of the assemblies."

Another asked, "How about the working height and the supplies for the assemblies?"

Greg's response was, "The height of the conveyor will be set so that assembly can be performed at the proper work height. Parts and supplies will be adjacent to the conveyor and hoist devices will be available."

Roger proceeded to discuss the plans on the new utilities mentioned earlier in the report. Members of the group listened with interest and by this time seemed to accept the concept.

Ed concluded with, "Are there any further questions or suggestions? Well, that's about it at this time. Ordinarily I would not bring the pilot upholstery line into our case goods plant. The move, if necessary, is only temporary. Now that we have worked out the style and manufacturing technology in the pilot line, we will ultimately be setting up that operation in another town.

"I'm sure there are many more things to be worked out in detailing the master plan. They will be taken up as work on the project goes forward. We will be getting together again over the next phase of the program."

FIGURE 5–4
Illustration, Layout Detail

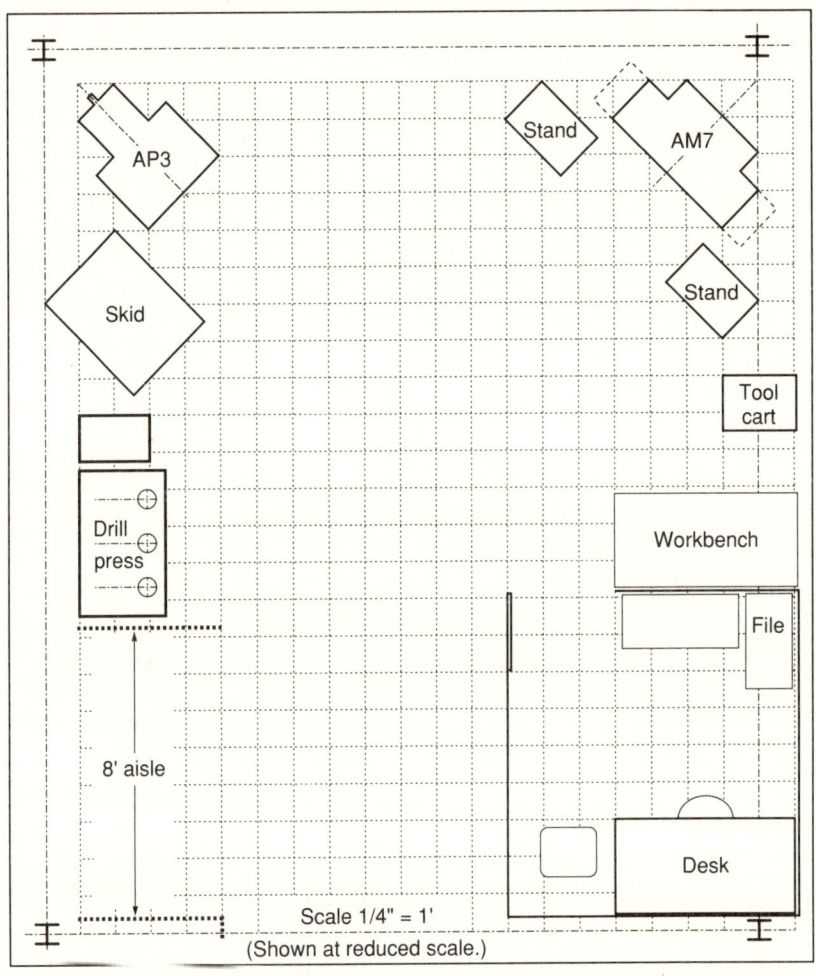

In the following period, a set of site and building plans was prepared for the new facility. A building permit was obtained from the town. The fact that the project included plans to improve the ecology of the adjacent river undoubtedly speeded approval of the plans. Greg set up a plan view of the building on mylar quadruled grid film. A scale of ¼ of an inch to the foot was selected for the layout. The building walls, columns, utilities, and other fixed structures were set in with pressure-sensitive tape or drawn on the matte surface of the mylar. Templates for each machine and facility were prepared.

The supervisor or manager of each section reviewed the details for that section as they became available. A typical illustration of the layout detail is shown in Figure 5–4. The locations of the machines are established, and the position can be read from the grid in the layout. Significant or critical dimensions are also drawn in on the layout.

Another meeting was held to review the complete detailed plant layout and discuss other aspects of the program. Questions were resolved about the forthcoming move of operations from the Grove Street plant. Ed noted that the program was fairly well on schedule. He suggested they have a mid-project shrimp dinner celebration at the River Road Tavern that night—an invitation to which no one objected.

The bulldozers had already worked over the site. The foundation was laid, and the riggers and all the other trades were at work on various sections of the building. In time, a proper completion ceremony was held with town officials in attendance. Ed arranged for the dedication of the small park provided by that gracious southern lady, Sue Bell.

As in many projects, some adjustments were made to the layout in the course of the program. It wasn't long before the conveyor assembly plan was working well. The company had taken a step to a higher level of productivity. In time, Ed moved into the corner office as president, with new duties and responsibilities.

CHAPTER SUMMARY

Value added to a product in manufacturing consists of fabrication and assembly work that is essential and uniquely deals with the product. Excess materials handling adds nothing to the product except indirect costs.

The pursuit of productivity and product quality has led companies to give increased attention to layout of facilities in work cells and according to the product fabrication/assembly sequence. This approach, coupled with two complementary procedures, can be very effective. The procedures include scheduling production to customer orders and ordering materials for delivery only when needed and in the quantities needed.

Both the layout and procedural aspects provide for:

- Reduced plant space requirements.
- Lower inventory cost.
- Quick reaction to quality problems.

The product assembly sequence, however, is only one of four concepts in layout planning. A functional (process) grouping of facilities by machine type is employed where the desire is to obtain the advantages of multiple machine assignment, efficient layout, and uniformity of the material delivery system. An example of this is the grouping of automatic screw machines in a single work center.

A third concept is to provide for complete construction and assembly of a product at a single location. The construction and assembly of very large products may be fabricated at a single location.

The fourth and newest approach consists of work-cell manufacturing layout, employing group technology. In this system, the group technology analysis identifies families of parts that can be produced in a work cell consisting of several machines serviced by one or more operators. Ultimately, each manufacturing cell is then arranged according to the general production manufacturing sequence. Most layouts evolve from some combination of the concepts, depending on the specific product and process factors.

Plant layout involves a comprehensive analysis of workflow, supporting services, utilities, materials handling, security, safety features, and other specialized requirements. The plans should be based on the planned production rate and staffing requirements. Provision should be made for both short-range internal expansion space and long-range external expansion of building.

Planners should prepare a set of specifications for the layout and building. They will also have to develop cost estimates and economic data to provide for project costing and control. In addition, project schedules will help monitor the progress of the work.

In approaching layout planning, it is important to devote a considerable amount of thought and work to developing general concepts and layout plans. At this stage, an opportunity exists to introduce new concepts and improvements over current layouts and operations. In the plans, provision should also be made for a next-stage expansion if that is anticipated at the site.

There is an organized approach that attempts to minimize materials handling between successive operations or work centers. The approach can be applied to either a composite (micro) product assembly process or a (macro) grouping of work centers by function. The general approach is as follows.

1. Flow of materials. Determine the sequence in the movement of materials between operations and/or work centers.
2. Activity relationships. Obtain a set of the indices of the (cost-related) volume of material movement between operations or work centers.
3. Operation/work center size requirements. Compute the physical space requirements for operations/work centers.
4. Relative location of operation/work centers. Arrange operation/work centers in relation to each other with regard to their size and relational importance—all within some acceptable configuration or actual building space.
5. General layout scheme. One or more general layout schemes can be used to seek agreement on a general layout. The drawing may also show the workflow, main

aisles, and other features not expressly treated in the analysis. The purpose at this stage is to assure understanding of the general plan, evaluate its merits, and ultimately obtain agreement on the general plan.

6. Detailed layout plan. Following acceptance of the general layout, the detailed layout of each work center and operation can be prepared and reviewed for subsequent approval. Approval should start from the bottom up (line supervisors to general management).

There are several computer programs that may aid in working through the analysis. Each of the programs has an array of different features. The analysis of workflow and materials handling is, however, only one of the many considerations. Electronic and high-tech industries require specialized facilities, such as a "clean-room," for the manufacturing process. Good facilities also help attract personnel and provide the atmosphere of "a good place to work."

CHAPTER 6

COST REDUCTION

The potential applications for cost reduction abound in business, industry, and the service sector. The federal government also has a large stake in the activity, considering the cost of acquiring goods and services.

One of the prime roles of an industrial or manufacturing engineer is production planning—an activity of fairly wide scope. As the process, tools, and layout are developed, it is presumed that the engineer will have selected the most economic method for the given factors. In time, changes will make the process obsolete. New capabilities will develop, production quantities may change, and other factors will dictate the need for replanning the manufacturing method. This situation provides an opportunity to reduce manufacturing cost.

Reducing cost is one of the most effective ways of increasing profitability. There are other approaches, like increasing prices (without loss in sales volume), increasing sales volume, or changing the product mix to more profitable lines. But all of these—mostly marketing decisions—have their drawbacks and limitations. Reducing manufacturing cost, on the other hand, can be an effective internally controlled approach in a competitive market.

VALUE ENGINEERING

There is an activity closely related to the subject of traditional cost reduction called *value engineering*. Although both subjects have many common elements, value engineering employs a somewhat special approach. The first phase is a fact-finding cost analysis of a part. The second phase, the judicial aspect, is a functional analysis consisting of a search for a lower-cost alternative to meeting the functional need of the part or assembly.

The technique features defining the function of a part by using two words only: a verb and a noun. For example, the function of a part may be described as: support—frame. Then the criterion is applied: The function is worth its cost only if there is no other acceptable way of performing the function at less cost. In working through the analysis, high-cost or redundant parts are revealed.

NARRATIVE: TED KIEL'S COMSYS COMPANY

When Ted Kiel's parents moved from Japan to the United States, they settled near the Silicon Valley in California. Ted went on to become a brilliant design engineer in the electronics field. In time, Ted got a company together named Comsys that designed and manufactured communication systems and hardware. Many of the applications were for aerospace and military programs requiring data acquisition and reduction utilizing telemetry products.

The product line consisted of devices for transmitting physical measurements to a remote recorder. They were designed like the "Cadillacs" of the industry. Since most of the business was for the military, performance, not cost, was the object.

Tony, the vice president of manufacturing, was left alone pretty much to run his show. He ran the manufacturing almost like a company within a company—sufficient unto itself. To paraphrase his approach, it was, "Just give me the design—I'll take care of the rest." On previous occasions, product design engineers had experienced some apparent resistance to answering questions about the fabrication of a part. While it was not a good situation, the designers would get a break from their boards and sometimes get a good idea while seeing other operations in the shop.

The business prospered during the period of heavy investment in military equipment. The plant had gone through several expansions. The purchasing department was pleased by obtaining low unit costs although the order size was large. But as a cutback in the military buildup occurred, the company got caught with an excessive inventory of parts and assemblies. Manufacturing had accumulated over two years' inventory of parts!

It became apparent that measures should be instituted to reduce cost. Ted suggested to Chi Chan, his manager of engineering, that he might wish to initiate a cost reduction program.

Chi thought about how he might proceed with the program. In considering the qualifications of his staff, Chi recalled that one of his employees, Jay Kerr, had a background in both electronic and industrial engineering. In talking to Jay about the assignment, he mentioned that he would like to limit the program to engineering product design considerations at this time. Chi went on to state that two other people from product design would be assigned to work with him. Gail, a new employee in product design, and Terry, one of the senior members of the department who was familiar with their product line, would be the other members of the group.

Several days later, Chi called the group together and suggested they start with the MPS-3 modulator unit. (A modulator is a device that changes the property of an electrical wave, called the carrier, in response to some property of another signal, called the modulating signal. AM and FM radio transmissions are examples of amplitude- and frequency-modulated transmissions, respectively.) The MPS-3 unit was about 4 inches wide by 2 inches high and 11 inches long. The unit plugged into one of their cabinet racks. Chi placed one of their MPS-3 modulators and a set of drawings of the unit on the table. He mentioned that Jay would be coordinating the work of the group and then turned the meeting over to him.

After a few preliminary remarks, Jay distributed copies of a data sheet form for the cost reduction program. The form (which will be illustrated later with data) listed the part number, name, number of pieces required per product, and the function and cost of the part.

Jay explained, "One of our initial tasks will be to obtain the data on the components of our MPS-3 unit. We can work from our indented parts list to pick off the components and subassemblies." Turning to Gail, Jay requested, "Gail, would you fill in the information for the part number, name, and number required per product on the form? Then when you have the parts listed, would you give Terry and me a copy?"

"Sure," Gail responded.

"Terry, would you do the functional analysis?" Jay inquired. Terry nodded his consent to the task. "I will get the cost data," stated Jay.

Continuing, Jay said, "At our next meeting we will have three items on the agenda: first, review data; second, identify more promising parts and subassemblies subject to cost reduction; and third, initiate, but not evaluate, design concepts that may reduce cost."

While this is how the cost reduction program started, some limitations in scope are evident. Before proceeding with the narrative, we will pursue a more general approach to the subject of cost reduction.

ORGANIZATION AND RESPONSIBILITY

From the organizational standpoint and the matter of responsibility, there are several different systems. One of the fairly common approaches employs some combination of a *staff and line responsibility*. Part of the regular duties of industrial and manufacturing engineers is to initiate and advance cost reduction cases. As noted earlier, the initial manufacturing planning should have provided for economic production processes, but new opportunities emerge. For companies that have an employee suggestion system, the proposals are usually evaluated by the engineer serving that particular department.

In another approach, *project teams* are employed that may be set up across organizational lines so that the best mix of talent is brought to bear on the specific project under development.

For very high-level organizational cost reduction, the analysis may be performed by the "special assistant to" *staffer, or a consultant* engaged for the study. The analysis may involve changing the organizational relationships to clarify and fix responsibility for achieving an operating cost reduction and the appropriate cost goals. The reorganization could go in either direction—from a functional organization to a product line or business type group or in the reverse direction. One of the effects should be to establish a manageable responsibility for the operating center.

Finally there is the crash-type *"arbitrary edict"* directive. In this case an order is issued: Cut all costs by 10 percent. This is a quick, broad-scale approach. Unless there is some vital long-term basis, the desired results may not persist. Substantial opportunities often require extensive analysis and planning. An edict may cut the wrong program and/or in the wrong department.

COST AND STANDARD DATA

The format of cost data varies from one company to another. Regardless of the system, it is essential to be able to determine the components of labor, material, and overhead (assigned at the department level) for each part and subassembly in discrete product industries and also for units of production in process industries. Isolating each factor highlights excess costs in an otherwise reasonable-appearing total cost. The elements of scrap and rework must be identifiable in cost reduction analysis.

PLANNING LEVELS

For cost reduction projects relating to parts or assemblies, information is essential on the quantities to be produced. Normally an annual planning level is required. Because the requirement or activity level typically varies throughout the year over the initial planning level, some companies base the evaluation on two indices: the annual planning level and the current requirement level. This helps in following up on the performance of major projects where the actual results may fall short of or exceed the expectations.

The evaluation of some cost reduction projects do not directly relate to components or production quantities of a single part. In these cases, the standard units of measurement for the process industry are employed. Commonly these units are length, weight, or volume.

PERSONNEL QUALIFICATIONS

As is the case for this and other development programs, it is important to provide good leadership. If some form of a group project is employed, a person should head the group who possesses a high degree of human relations skills along with evident enthusiasm and energy to carry out the program.

Members of the group can be notably different in their backgrounds and qualifications. Desirable traits, though in varying degrees, will certainly include analytical and technical talent, practical judgment, and creativity.

PROJECT SELECTION

Because the potential areas are so extensive, one of the initial steps is to identify and select the more promising area or application on which to focus. While all departments of an organization would hardly be discouraged from reducing cost, it becomes a question of focusing on the area or activity that has the greatest impact on profitability and return on investment.

The first step, therefore, in approaching the task is to establish some index or ranking of the more promising areas or applications. To accomplish this, experienced judgments can be made on the percentage improvement that may be obtainable in different areas or projects and the subsequent saving and effects on profitability. As an example, for a plastics plant, a potential 7 percent change in the extrusion rate may improve profitability by 14 percent, while an 11 percent change in delivery cost may only affect profitability by 6 percent, and so on. Thus by arranging the potential projects in the form of a Pareto curve, attention can be focused on the more profitable projects.

Another term used to describe the approach with the same objective is to make a *profit sensitivity analysis*. Employing this, one examines the effect on profitability of an arbitrary or nominal percentage change in some factor of the various applications under consideration. In essence, the approach is a matter of selecting one or more of the leading potential cost reduction projects.

Sometimes meritorious cost reduction cases just emerge from the suggestion of an operator in the shop doing the job or from a reevaluation of the process by the manufacturing engineer responsible for the process plan.

PROJECT EXECUTION

A favorable climate should be created for ideas and new concepts. An idea that is not practical may lead to another one that is useful.

After all analysis, the cost reduction will more than likely involve changes. These have to be sold! A good relationship involving line managers with staff support will facilitate bringing the programs to a successful conclusion.

> The group, Jay, Gail, and Jerry, got together for the second meeting in the small engineering conference room. Each member brought his or her set of the cost reduction data sheets along with other material that might be necessary.
> In comparing notes on their findings, it was apparent that to be able to complete the data sheets, two tasks remained. First, in order to deal with actual parts and

subassemblies, they would have to prepare manufacturing bills of material (like indented parts lists), as some manufacturing subassemblies existed for which the engineering materials list had not assigned parts numbers. Second, they would have to break down or develop cost information for a number of parts where plant cost figures only listed the cost of the subassembly.

Jay spoke up first, saying, "OK, let's dig into this," and in the following half hour, Jay, Gail, and Terry were able to complete the data sheet form shown in Figure 6–1.

After a short coffee break, Jay resumed with, "Now we come to the fun part—concepts, ideas, and 'imagineering.' The ground rules for the balance of this session are as follows: We are now seeking ideas for cost reduction—but with the provision that no attempt should be made to evaluate or challenge the idea at this time. We are just seeking a free flow of ideas."

Jay continued with, "As you know, the present design of the chassis consists of three milled sides which are screwed together. After the PC card is mounted to stand-offs, the top cover and the back and front plates are attached to complete the unit.

"To get the ball rolling on ideas, here's a concept: Change the chassis design from a built-up box assembly to an extruded U shape. The PC card and the top cover could be held in a channel in the extrusion." Jay picked up a piece of chalk and sketched the design concept on the white board as shown in Figure 6–2. The group went on to discuss the idea, but under the ground rules no one attempted to evaluate the concept at this time.

Gail came up with, "How about changing the top cover design, which is now machined, to a stamped part? That should reduce the cost."

Jerry observed, "In the course of this work, we should consider replacing our assorted locking and ejecting devices for each modulator with standard commercially available devices. Over the years, we have accumulated half a dozen different designs where one standard unit could be used."

FIGURE 6-1
Data Sheet, Cost Reduction Program

Product: MPS-3 Modulator			Planning Level: 2,000 units/yr.		
Part (or Assembly Number)	Name/ Description	No. Req. per Product	Function	Cost/ Part ($)	Notes
7005	Chassis	1	Protect, support PC card	11.07	
7017	Trim	1	Enhance appearance	1.84	
7029	Cover	1	Protect PC card	5.72	

FIGURE 6–2
Extrusion Design Concept

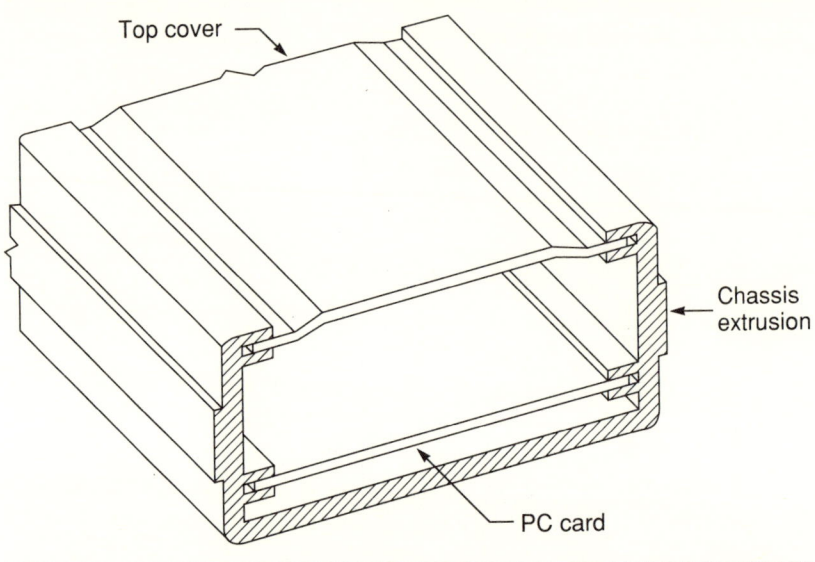

The group advanced several other ideas, after which Jay stated, "Well, we have a number of ideas to work on and develop for our meeting next week at this time. Thanks, see you then."

The group met again to develop and refine the various concepts. Chi, the engineering manager, dropped in to check on the program. He could see that the group was making progress. Chi mentioned that, while attention was initially focused on the MPS-3 modulator, this was only one of a family of four similar products in that line. And therefore, they might wish to expand the scope of their attention to cost reduction changes that would apply to the whole four products in the line.

The fourth meeting consisted of an intensive screening of the concepts and design sketches against three criteria:

1. Technical feasibility, consistent with product function.
2. Economic merit.
3. Market appearance and meeting design standards.

Detail drawings had been prepared for the leading new design under consideration. Cost data were obtained for each part and subassembly. The proposed design change that was applicable to all four units of the modulator line consisted of the U-shaped extrusion chassis with provision for a slide-in PC card and top cover, as shown earlier in Figure 6–2.

The single extrusion would take the place of the present three parts which required milling, drilling, and assembly operations. Jerry raised the question about possible warping of the U-shaped extrusion, but the vendor assured the group that a properly designed die and process control would provide an extrusion section within the required tolerances.

The project group also checked out an alternate possibility. A design in which only two sides were extruded and similar top and bottom covers were spot welded would also provide an attractive cost reduction.

The next step was to calculate the saving for the design change that applied to the modulator line. The calculation is shown in Figure 6–3. The cost of amortizing the extrusion die was factored into the part cost. The analysis revealed a saving of $50,000–indeed attractive for the proposal.

Management gave prompt approval for the design change. Consideration was given both to the life of the product and the current inventory position. In successive meetings, the group went on to several other applications of cost reduction and continued to follow up on the extrusion design to assure success of the project.

In one case, Gail uncovered operational problems at the console in which one of many similar modulator units was installed. She learned that confusion sometimes occurs when an operator adjusts a potentiometer of one modulator while mistakenly reading the dial of the adjacent modulator. To solve this problem, Gail suggested moving the associated control and instrument dial on each modulator closer together and enclosing the control and dial with a $1/8$-inch colored silk-screened band. While not contributing to cost reduction, this idea improved operator control and market appeal.

Throughout the course of the program, the members of the group had to dig for much of the information that was

FIGURE 6-3
Calculation of Saving

Change	Description	Cost		Unit Saving	Annual Saving
		Present Design	Proposed Design		
	Products: Modulator Line		Planning Level: 8,000 units/yr.		
1	Change from machined chassis assembly to extruded design. (Material, parts, fabrication, assembly, and hardware.)	$11.07	$ 7.35		
2	Change from machined top cover to a stamped part. (Material, parts, fabrication, assembly, and hardware.)	5.72	3.19		
	Total	$16.79	$10.54	$6.25	$50,000

necessary to evaluate the cost reduction concepts. There was nothing wrong with that—it was part of their work. However, it became apparent to members of the group that the application of cost reduction would be facilitated by having ready access to essential data. The group prepared a report that included a set of recommendations. The recommendations were as follows:

1. Set up a standard data base that would be made available to engineering on the current and annual planning level across product lines.
2. Develop a parts data base that provides information on the commonality of parts and assemblies across product lines.

FIGURE 6–4
General Cost-Reduction Applications

Product Design

Design Simplification
- Simplify concept that meets function.
- Reduce number of parts.

Design Extension
- Extend features of part to serve more functions.

Material Substitution
- Use lower-cost material or process meeting function.

Standardization
- Use commercially available parts where feasible for lower cost and shorter lead time.

Manufacturing Engineering

Manufacturing Planning
- Plan economic process plan, methods, and workplace.

Manufacturing Layout and Materials Handling
- Develop efficient layout.

Facilities and Equipment
- Provide productive machine tools.

Automation
- Automate process where feasible and economic.

Quality Control
- Provide engineering support to manufacturing.

Cost Reduction
- Make periodic review of applications.

Manufacturing and Other Functions

Supervision and Training
- Provide good training and supervision.

Material Control
- Develop effective system, check application of JIT.

Purchasing
- Seek timely and cost-effective acquisition with JIT.

Maintenance
- Utilize preventive maintenance system.

Quality Control
- Maintain effective quality control.

Accounting
- Seek effective cost system and control.

The data base should provide information on standard cost of parts and actual manufacturing assemblies.

3. Distribute the information on scrap and rework to engineering for review and follow-up.

4. Introduce a suggestion system so that operators in the shop have an organized and supported means of suggesting improvements.

In addition to the above recommendations, the group included a chart, shown in Figure 6–4, on the general means of obtaining cost reduction.

In time, the development work of the group was expanded to include all staff and line people in the company. Substantial cost reduction and increased productivity were realized. This enabled the company to expand its product line and obtain a larger share of the commercial market.

CHAPTER SUMMARY

Reducing cost is one of the most effective ways of increasing profitability. The closely related subject of value engineering similarly seeks to reduce cost by obtaining the lowest cost design that meets the requirements for the function of the part or assembly.

The responsibility and organization for cost reduction may employ some combination of line and staff members, special project teams, a staffer or consultant, or an arbitrary edict to reduce cost by a given percentage. Regardless of the system, it is essential to be able to determine the components of labor, material, and overhead assigned at the department level. Information on production planning levels is also essential.

Personnel qualifications include well-developed human relations skills, analytical and technical talent, practical judgment, and creativity. In approaching the task, it is essential to focus on the more promising and profitable applications for cost reduction warranting the investment of time and talent.

Potential applications for cost reduction extend through all functions, including engineering design, manufacturing engineering, manufacturing, accounting, and sales. To foster, support, and control cost reduction, management should provide an organized cost reduction and suggestion system in the organization. Timely action should be taken in follow-up on shop suggestions in support of the program.

CHAPTER 7

TECHNICAL ANALYSIS

There are occasions in most companies when a very special problem develops in a manufacturing plant that requires a highly focused technical analysis. While this happens throughout all kinds of industries, it more frequently happens in situations where the technology is pressed to the limit of manufacturing capability. Sometimes the process works without our fully understanding why. And what is equally mystifying—the problem may go away without anybody knowing why. But with care and diligence, an analyst can track down most problems.

The types of problems stretch the imagination. A case in point: In the early days of vacuum tube manufacture at a leading plant, the gold grid flashing process became irregular. It was discovered that during lunch time, an operator was toasting her cheese sandwiches in the gold flashing oven! Not all solutions are as readily discovered or as easily solved.

An analyst may be called upon to work on diverse problems. It could be an operating system problem such as production control, or it might be technical trouble shooting on a fabrication problem. To be effective, competence in the subject area is presumed—but there is much more. The possession of a creative curiosity is an asset. If the problem involves people (as most do), it is essential to be able to work well with other associates during the analysis and ultimate solution.

A given statement of the problem can be misleading or only partly correct. Recall, as described in the chapter on material control systems, that while the problem was reported to be in the production control department, other departments also contributed to the difficulties. The system was working until an unprecedented sales demand developed. But it's hard to call an increase in sales a problem!

Or, to take another example: A major NC milling machine was acquired and for several years produced acceptable parts. But gradually over a period of five years, the yield dropped to 59 percent, with long down times and high-cost supplier service. What was the problem? Was it the machine, or operator, or what? Well, although the machine was prematurely worn out and obsolete, discontinued by the manufacturer, and so sensitive that a mild tap on the controller box would cause the table to jump two inches, the decision to replace the machine "could not" be made. The unit had been given a 12-year life, of which only 5 years were charged against depreciation. In this case, no amount of technical analysis and trouble shooting (even by the manufacturer's representative) could fix the problem. Cast another way, the problem could be viewed as a machine-life judgment call, the resolution of which certainly affected profitability. *Deferring a share of profits for long-range productivity is becoming recognized as good management strategy!*

The nature of a problem and its cause can be viewed differently from the technical and managerial standpoints. Understandably, an engineer will focus on the technology, while a manager may also consider personnel as part of the problem and/or solution. The ultimate resolution of a problem is usually determined by some combination of factors including technical, personnel, resources, and the management of the development program.

The following narrative program deals with technical analysis of a hinge manufacturing process. The reader might well ask, "What does this have to do with the specifics of my work?" The answer is, while the details may be coincidental, the more general value lies in illustrating the need to dig down into the specifics of the technology. Each industrial problem is always just a little bit different from all others. The difference has to be evaluated and the appropriateness of the solution has to be determined. *There is a need for excellence in technology as well as in management.*

NARRATIVE: HOME NOVELTY PRODUCTS COMPANY

The role of CEO had been passed on to Margo, the daughter of the founder of the Home Novelty Products Company. The company had recently relocated to the suburbs of a large eastern city. Its product line consisted of high-style notebooks and other novelty items. The products were mostly made of paper, plastic, and cardboard, along with metal parts where required. For years the company prospered with its manufacturing and sales organizations. When a problem developed, they would try to work it out in the shop, talk to a vendor, or occasionally call someone in to solve the problem, since they had no engineer in the company.

The company had introduced a very attractive line of photo albums. The binding consisted of a series of very thin, interlocking metal hinges made of a gold-colored anodized aluminum. Photographers would often choose the albums for wedding pictures because of the elegant gold appearance of the binding and cover of the album.

Margo seemed to sense an increasing number of technical problems emerging as their product line and plant operations expanded. The people in the plant knew a lot about the handling of paper, its grain, and other properties, but they were dependent upon vendors for metal and plastic parts. Margo decided to hire an engineer to work on technical problems that kept emerging in the company.

As Eric, the new project engineer, was settling into his office, he received a call from Margo, "Eric, would you come to my office?"

"Sure," replied Eric.

Eric noticed the door was open and caught Margo's eye, at which time she said, "Come in." As Eric tried to keep from sinking too deeply in the leather-lined chair, Margo finished signing some papers. Looking up she said, "Eric, I would like you to take as your first assignment, the solution of the gold hinge problem. We have been buying the hinge from a vendor in New Jersey, but they are having trouble making the part. If you want to arrange a visit to the vendor, check with Matt, our materials manager. In addition, I told Kurt, our manufacturing manager, that you would probably be coming down to go over our hinge assembly process here in the plant." Margo reached over and handed a sample of the hinge to Eric. At that point Margo's phone rang. Just before Margo picked up the phone she said, "Thank you, Eric."

Back in his office, Eric looked over the part and then called Matt about the hinge problem. Matt was anxious to discuss the problem because the inventory of stock, even though of marginal quality, was getting very low. Eric's first question was, "Matt, could I have a copy of the drawing of the part?"

Matt's response was, "Oh well, we don't have a drawing of the hinge. We just contracted for the manufacture of the part to a vendor, the Classic Hinge Company. We told them what we wanted, and they said they could make it. What they actually did was subcontract the fabrication of the part to another company, the MicroTool Company, a tool and die shop. It's located about 30 miles from Classic."

Eric thanked Matt for the background and mentioned that he would like to visit the MicroTool plant where the hinge is fabricated. He then went down into the factory area, where he found Kurt. Kurt led Eric to the hinge assembly process. After observing the process for a short time, Kurt was called away on some other matter. In brief, the process involved bonding the aluminum hinge to a cardboard strip and subsequently bonding the cardboard strip to the photo page holder. Ultimately, the hinge pages are assembled by inserting hinge pins that hold adjacent pages and the front and back panels of the album. All this was interesting, but did not advance the solution of the problem at the vendor's plant.

The defects in the hinge were noticeable with the naked eye. Instead of a uniformly rounded knuckle, irregular flat sections were evident. These not only made it difficult to insert the hinge pin but also detracted from the appearance and marketability of the album. Back in his office, Eric picked up a loupe from his small tool collection in the bottom drawer. Fixing the loupe in his eye, he looked at the hinge more closely. He could see the sharp lines in the knuckles of the

FIGURE 7–1
Illustration of Hinge

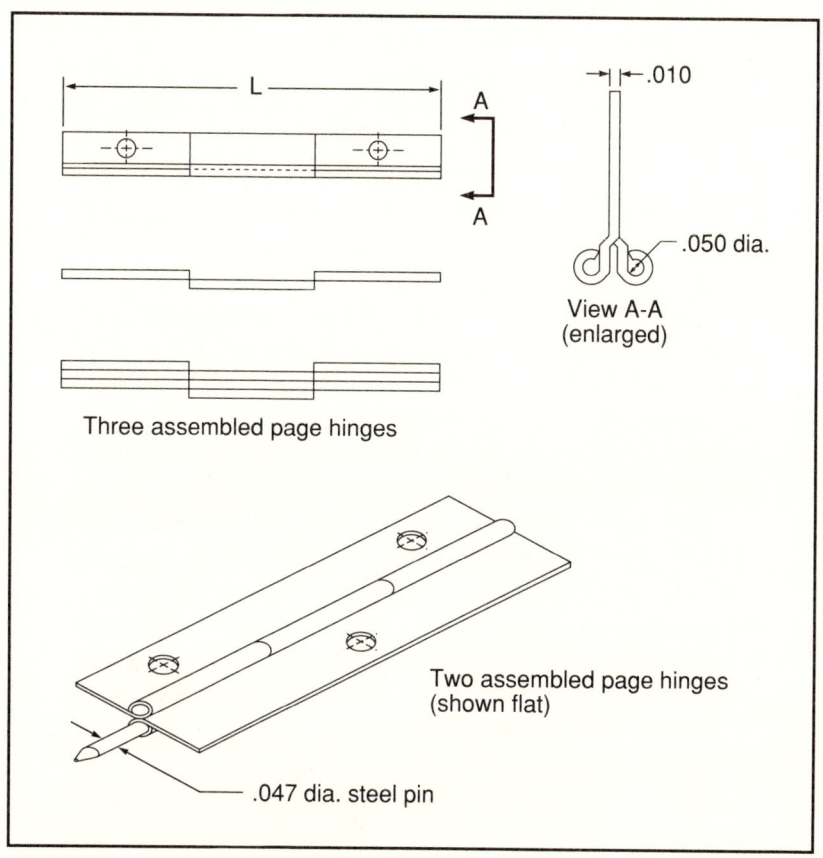

"L" length, in 3, 5, 9, and 11 inches.
Material: .010 anodized aluminum alloy (alloy to be specified).
Note: For simplicity, some details are omitted in this illustration.

hinge where whole sections were flat instead of round. Eric got out his micrometer and other small tools in order to take measurements of the hinge. After a considerable amount of checking, he prepared a drawing of the hinge. A simplified illustration is shown in Figure 7–1.

Some of the things Matt said on the way to the Classic Hinge Company with Eric indicated some frustrations in managing materials. He mentioned that occasionally he was called in on problems with parts, for which he had little or no background. Matt was glad to have technical support on the selection and acquisition of piece parts.

Matt introduced Eric to the general manager of Classic Hinge, who in turn called Jeff, their purchasing agent, who accompanied Matt and Eric to MicroTool. In the lobby of MicroTool were several display cases showing their precision components, including the photo album hinge, the production of which was in trouble.

Jeff introduced Matt and Eric to Larry, the head of the tool and die shop. Larry stated, "We ran into some bad sheet stock. Classic Hinge orders the material for us. They say it's hard to get the same grade of material from jobbers."

At that point Eric spoke up, "Could either of you, Larry or Jeff, talk about the process and routing of the material before it gets here?"

Jeff, from Classic Hinge, spoke up, "Well, we order the rolled stock from a jobber. Then it's sent to a Pennsylvania shop where it gets anodized. They don't have a slitting machine, so the material is then sent to a slitter, where it gets slit and rewound onto coils about half an inch wide. The large coils are then sent here to MicroTool, where the hinge is fabricated. We, at Classic, can heat-treat the stock and are trying some of it on an experimental basis."

Larry spoke up, "Would you like to see the operation in our shop?" "Yes," all agreed. As the group approached the operation, Larry hailed Joe, the setup man, and asked him if he would start up the press. Joe commented that he had just made an adjustment and that it was OK to start up the operation.

The part was fabricated in a punch press, operating a progressive die. The stock advanced two inches for each stroke of the press. In the first station, a notch and a pilot hole are punched in the stock. The pilot hole is used by subsequent stations to register and align the strip in each successive station. In turn, sections of the strip are partially slit and partially offset; then the knuckle is preformed; and finally the knuckle is finished formed, after which the strip is cut to the prescribed length.

Shortly after the press was started, it was shut down for another adjustment. The square, malformed knuckles were still evident on the hinge. At that point, Eric asked for and obtained a sample of the initial start-up strip from the press run.

The meeting ended without a conclusion as to the specifics of the problem or the solution. MicroTool mentioned that a new supply of stock was on the way. As work on the program continued, the action taking place at MicroTool was to try one material after another, with various heat treatments, in an attempt to find a combination that would produce a satisfactory part. Clearly, a trial-and-error approach was being employed.

Everyone often uses the trial-and-error (or test) method. However, it's hard to argue against going directly to the solution, if possible. The engineer or manager seeks to employ all knowledge applicable to the problem. In the development presented, since the technology of coldworking is well established, a direct approach was possible.

Back in his office, Eric went to the heart of the matter. His plan was to:

1. Analyze what actually happens to the material in the process.
2. Select a material that has the properties that would make it suitable for the cold-working process.

In undertaking the first step, Eric examined the start-up strip from the press run, showing each operation as the hinge is formed in each stage of the progressive die. He then went back to MicroTool to examine the concept, drawings, and precision of the progressive die used in making the hinge. The result of Eric's physical analysis is shown in Figure 7–2.

The physical analysis shown in Figure 7–2 reveals each operation in the sequence and the behavior of the material as the knuckles become malformed during the process. In essence, during the coldworking of the material, stress builds up until an abrupt deformation occurs at the point of maximum bending stress. The material does not bend

FIGURE 7-2
Physical Analysis of Hinge Formation

Operations	Malformed Knuckles	Proper Knuckle Formation
1A. Start preform	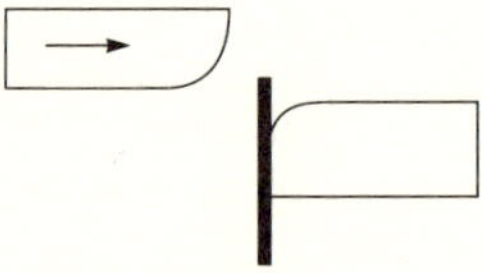	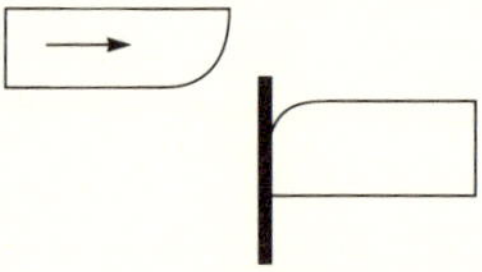
1B. Finish preform	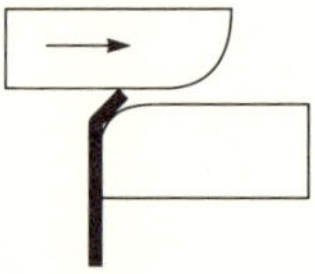	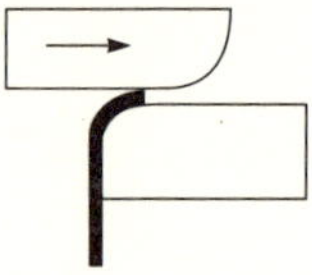
2A. Start knuckle form	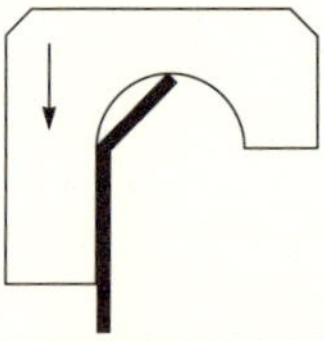	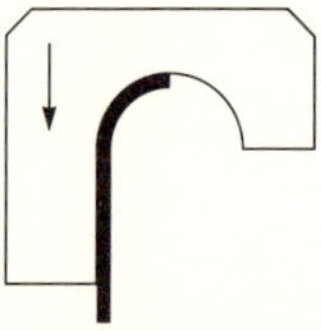
2B. Continue knuckle form	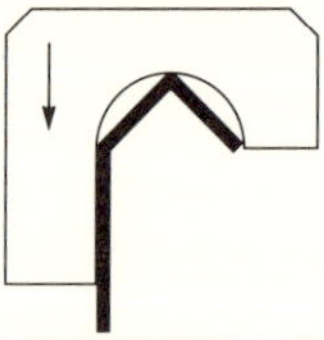	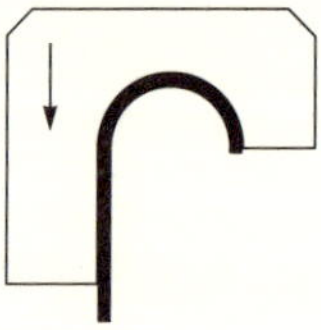
2C. Finish knuckle form	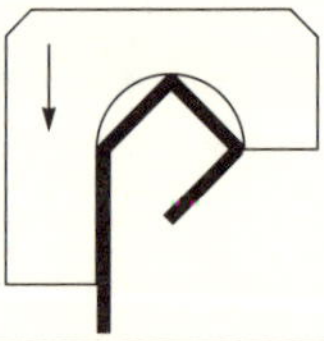	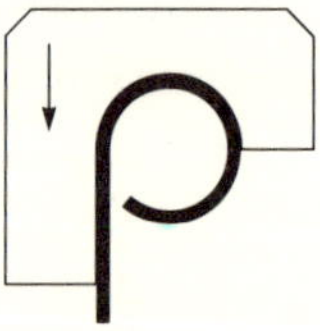

uniformly as shown in the adjacent column under proper knuckle formation.

There is another aspect to the analysis—the material itself. The material is an anodized aluminum alloy only

0.010 inch thick. (We will discuss the subject of specific alloys and their properties shortly.) Since the material is very thin, the anodized surface produces a subtle effect. Even though the anodized surface penetration was on the order of 0.0001 inch, the effect is to produce a kind of outer layer stiffening of the material.

Eric next turned to the matter of selecting an aluminum alloy with the required properties for forming the hinge. He knew that the leading factors relevant to the metal-working operation included: tensile strength, elongation, and hardness of the metal. Eric set forth the following specifications for the aluminum alloy:

Tensile strength:
  Ultimate: 22,000 psi or over
  Yield: 20,000 psi or over
  Spread: ultimate to yield, 1,000 or more
Elongation: 6 percent or more
Hardness: 40 or more (10 mm ball, 500 Kg F)

Eric felt that an aluminum alloy with these properties would provide for a considerable amount of bending without breaking and yet possess sufficient hardness to withstand the forces imposed both in the forming operation and in subsequent product handling.

Picking up a standard reference book on the properties of aluminum alloys, Eric started searching for an alloy that would meet the specifications. The alloy designated as number 3005-H32 was selected. The properties of this alloy are shown in Figure 7-3.

Having selected the material for the hinge, Eric turned the specification of the alloy over to Matt, the materials manager. Matt proceeded to contact the vendor, Classic Hinge, with the request to obtain the specified material. By this time, the buyers for major department stores were questioning Home Novelty Products on their ability to fill orders for photo albums for the holiday season.

The urgency of the matter became the number one priority in the plant. During his follow-up, Matt learned that

FIGURE 7–3
Properties of Aluminum Alloy Selected

Alloy	Tensile Strength (psi × 1,000)		Elongation (% in 2")	Hardness 10 mm Ball 500 Kg F	Application
	Ultimate	Yield			
3005-H32	25	21	6	40	A manganese alloy of moderate strength and excellent workability

the vendor was unable to locate a supply of the material. He then offered to assist them in obtaining the proper hinge material—an offer they accepted.

Matt went to Eric's office to discuss the problem. During the discussion, Eric suggested contacting Margo on the matter. Eric's idea was that contact between company presidents might get more action. Matt talked to Margo and her response was, "Sure, I'll get the supply house to move on this."

Within two weeks, the material (anodized and slit) was ready for the press. With considerable anxiety, the press set-up was made and the operation started. Success! The hinge formed properly as planned.

There was still something Eric had to do. To assure continued high-quality fabrication of the hinge, Eric prepared the trouble-shooting chart shown in Figure 7–4. While the key to solving the problem was analyzing the requirements and selecting the proper material, the tooling and setup also had to be properly maintained. The chart listed defects, causes, and the corrective action to be taken.

The tale could have ended here, but it did not. As a result of Eric's work on the hinge project, he found that the hinge was the highest-cost item of the photo album, and the anodizing process represented the major share of the material cost. In exploring alternatives, Eric located a gold-colored,

FIGURE 7–4
Hinge Trouble-Shooting Chart

Product Defects	Cause(s)	Solution(s)
1. Box-type knuckles with flat sections	Material too hard	Check material, replace if required
2. Burrs, malformation	Feed problem, improper registration	Check setup, feed, and registration
	Tools dull	Regrind tools
3. Camber	Low material clamping	Check clamping force
	Stock too narrow	Check, scrap if required
	Material too soft	Check hardness, replace if required
	Excessive friction	Check lubrication
4. Random defects in knuckles	Stray free burrs, slivers of aluminum	Clean tooling, check registration and feed
5. Defects in alternate knuckles	Alternate tooling not functioning properly	Check alternate tooling

vinyl-coated aluminum alloy material for the hinge. The material could be fabricated equally well into the hinge for the photo album. In addition, sales preferred the gold vinyl-coated hinge. While solving the initial problem, the development also reduced the cost of the part by 65 percent. The use of this material improved the quality and appearance of the product, along with representing an improvement in productivity for the company.

CHAPTER SUMMARY

Technical analysis is an exacting pursuit in the given field of application. To be effective, competence in the subject and the ability to work well with other associates during the analysis and development are essential.

Each analysis must pursue the particulars of the subject, looking for the unique factors in each situation. If, for example, the problem deals with the fabrication of material, seek to understand the physical, chemical, and/or electrical events taking place in and on the material. Consider: What does the material experience? Understanding that will often lead to determining what is required to correct the problem.

In systems work, seek to undertake a sufficiently broad scope of analysis to assure an adequate understanding of the problem. Seek to gain the participation and support of the people who will be affected. Since needs will change in time, look for adjustments that may be required.

CHAPTER 8

ADVANCE MANUFACTURING PLANNING

The previous chapters have presented material on current manufacturing technology. Narrative accounts have shown some of the problem areas along with development programs in responding to specific needs. While present systems are being upgraded and realigned, other developments are taking place. Advance manufacturing planning groups are developing concepts of the future factory. Where is all of this technology headed? What is the impact of computers, automation, and robots as we move closer to the concept of the future factory?

In Arthur C. Clarke's *July 20, 2019, Life in the 21st Century*, he writes, "The factory of 2019 won't have humans on the production lines. The factory of the future will resemble a more sophisticated version of Japan's Fujitsu Fanuc factory, where a hundred robots and only sixty humans produce ten thousand electric motors every month."[1]

Well, all this sounds interesting, and some of it is materializing. For many people—students, factory and office workers, engineers and managers—the implications are evident. A form of *future shock*[2] in regard to the future factory is upon us. I leave it to the sociologists to develop the full scenario.

In regard to machines and automated machine systems—even those with self-correcting artificial intelligent controllers—a machine will still need servicing, it will wear out and ultimately become operationally, technically, and economically obsolete. No one has found a way to violate the laws of physics. Friction and wear still occur. If something seems to defy the laws, we just haven't understood the principles well enough. Further, economics (present-worth principles on the time value of money) is ever present in making decisions on investment in machines and technology.

This chapter presents a conceptual synthesis of automation planning. A rationale is presented for converting a manual manufacturing system to an automated concept. In the process several useful design parameters are developed. We shall get to this shortly but first several general comments are presented about automation.

GENERAL CONCEPTS

Preliminary Considerations

Before undertaking an automation project, there are several preliminary considerations. A cursory walk through a manufacturing plant may reveal several operations that appear archaic and inefficient. But, without the background on the job, it is not appropriate to prejudge the process. Several preliminary considerations should be undertaken in evaluating the potential for automating the operation or process:

1. Is the design of the part stable, and what is the expected life?
2. What is the annual planning level and the demand throughout the year?
3. Should the part be redesigned to facilitate automated fabrication?
4. What are the expected difficult parts of the project?
5. Does economic analysis indicate an attractive return on investment?
6. Is this a candidate for a fixed (hard), versus flexible, manufacturing scheme?

Prove-Out Concept

The task of automating a process involves considerable investment with some inherent risk as to the performance of the machine or machine system. In view of this, it is generally advisable to commit an initial prove-out investment of up to about 10 percent of the expected total project cost. The initial step is to identify the most difficult part of the process or concept, then test it and prove it is feasible.

This amounts to taking a hard look at where one or more problems are likely to occur. There is an apt comment, "The job of an engineer is to find the fly in the ointment, while the job of a research scientist is to find the gold nugget in a pan of gravel."[3] Testing or proving feasibility is performed by modeling.

A distinction may be made between two different aspects. One is the question about the practical (physical) aspects of an operation or process. The other matter concerns the operational aspects. The operational aspects of large complex manufacturing systems can be tested with simulation software. (This will be discussed in the next chapter.) An analysis on the performance of the system is helpful in understanding and improving the behavior of the system.

Automation Inputs

In planning for the automation of some function or process, it is essential to understand and know the full characteristics of the inputs to the machine or system. This story will illustrate the pitfalls. During the initial sales negotiations on a project, the sales person for an automation design and construction company requested samples of parts that were to be packed into nested containers by the automated system. The plant manager for whom the system was being designed told one of his operators: "Go out and get some *good* parts!" The parts were ultimately passed on to the machinery designers of the automated system with the comment: "We are told the length of the parts in the process will not vary by more than ±1/16 inch." As the reader might anticipate, when the machinery was designed, built, installed, and test-run in the plant, some of the parts varied from 1 inch to 1 ¾ inches in length. Fortunately the upstream process could subsequently be brought into regulation within the original specifications.

Or suppose you are designing a machine to preset nails in a plastic wall box. What is the statistical distribution on the length, diameter, and upset head? How straight is the nail? How about the surface roughness—can it be slightly rusty? What is the contract with the vendor of the parts? The gears of the machine will methodically operate the machine cycle, but can the product handling components deal with the range of inputs to its system? In contrast to Gertrude Stein's often cited expression,[4] the converse in a different idiom might be: A nail is not a nail, is not a nail, is not a nail!

Personnel Aspects

As in all developments that are going to involve people, the manner in which human interaction is conducted and dealt with has a considerable bearing on the success of the venture. Friendly businesslike relationships with people in the shop should be maintained regardless of changes in the technology. In commenting about the difference between an automated plant in Japan and one in Detroit, Steve Cohen says ". . . that was the big change. In the way the people who work there were treated."[5]

AN AUTOMATION SYNTHESIS

In much of current manufacturing, islands of automation occur at one or more positions in the process. Where this occurs, the conditions have been favorable to design and build an automated machine or line for one or more operations on one or more parts. Factors like the configuration and production rate of the machine may have been determined by optional factors without regard to system considerations. With continued automation, a crossover point is reached, at which time the operation, cycle time, staffing, and equipment should be based on an integrated system concept.

This material presents a rationale for converting a manual/machine manufacturing system to an automated system concept. Aside from the question of technical and economic feasibility at this time, there are several important results that can be obtained from this approach, namely:

1. An indication of the kinds and number of operating devices that will be required.
2. A future design specification objective for the automated cycle time, based on an integrated system.
3. An indication of the production rate of the system.
4. Identification of associated equipment that will be required.
5. A guide for planning future developments.
6. Indication of desirable product design modifications to accommodate the automated process.

The rationale can be applied to any sequential discrete assembly process. In this illustration, the product consists of the assembly of a garment, more specifically a shirt. One of the special aspects of the apparel industry is that it is style-conscious. Other industries that have automated, including metal working, electronics, and process industries, are style-conscious but not style-restrictive. In this respect, it suggests that needle-trades automation should be of the flexible form with numerical control for the operating path.

The subject of automation in the apparel industry suggests another question. Why not consider nonwoven garments instead of going from thread to fabric to cutting to sewing assembly? Similarly, other thermal methods of joining material often employ a simulated stitch pattern because customers prefer it. This, of course, is a marketing factor.

In presenting the following material, the objective is to convey the general steps in the process. The form of the schematic drawings is presented, but only with sufficient detail necessary to convey the concepts.

Application of the Rationale

The rationale presented applies to the following general conditions:

1. The process consists of discrete component operations and assemblies.
2. The manufacturing of the product consists of a well-defined process.
3. The manual/machine operation times are well established and stable.
4. In this example, the unit operations are of the same kind (sewing), although they could be different if treated as such.
5. The analysis admits three classes of operations: automatic, semiautomatic, and manual.

Steps in the Process

Operation Flowchart—Present Process
Prepare an operation flowchart for the present process. This is illustrated in Figure 8–1. The chart shows only two branches of the complete process consisting of 51 sewing operations in making the garment. The manual process charted is described as an operation flowchart, as it shows operations in sequence that must be performed to make the product. The number of identical machines at each station that would be required for balanced workflow in the present manual system (Figure 8–1) are not shown. These are determined later, based upon an

FIGURE 8-1
Operation Flowchart

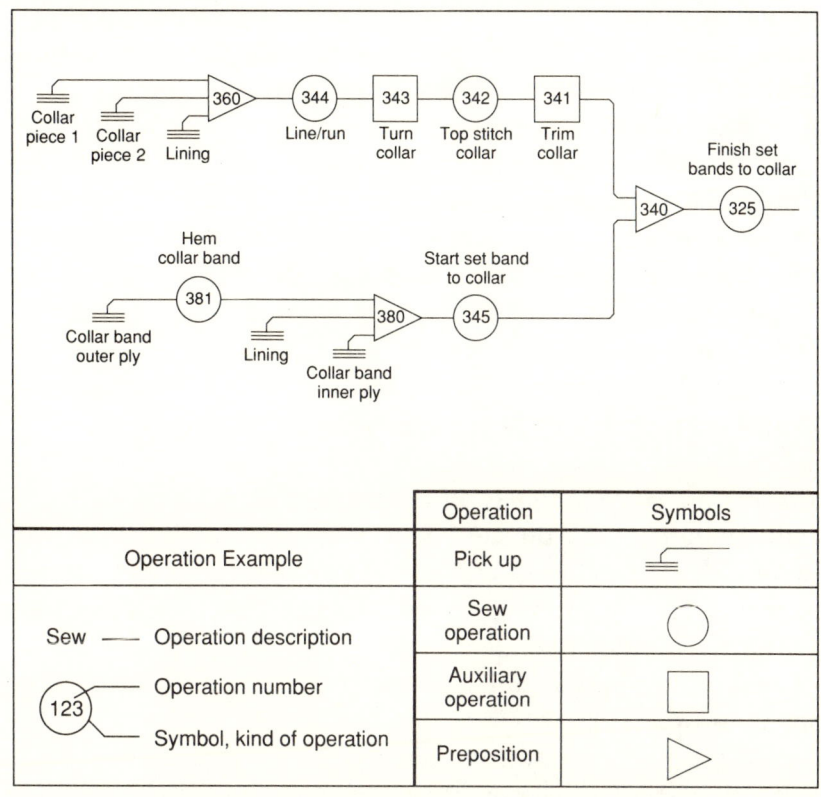

equivalent production rate that would match the automated system.

Each symbol in Figure 8-1 represents a discrete operation, machine, and/or function which must be performed. Note that assembly operations are symbolized by a circle and auxiliary operations with fixtures are characterized by a square. As will be shown later, operations can, of course, be classified as potential automatic, semiautomatic, or manual (not yet considered suitable for automation).

Transport devices between operations are implied but not symbolized. Two situations can be visualized in getting work from one station to another. It is possible for a machine to perform an operation and then move the part to a separate transport device, having a cycle time equal to the operation time. Alternately, it is possible to transfer the part immediately from an end operation to the next operating station.

Situations may exist when either one or the other scheme may be desirable, depending upon the individual operation time and the size and difficulty of moving the part. It is possible that orientation of the piece part could be performed during a move between operations. Preposition devices are shown for registering two or more piece parts. Refinement on these concepts can be considered in more detail in a later stage of the conceptual development. In this analysis, a small allowance for transfer time between stations is added to each cycle time.

Cycle Time and Balancing Worksheet

Fundamental to the development of an automated production system concept is the assignment of a cycle time for each operation that can be automated and the creation of line balance within the system. *Line balance* refers to the planned equalization of workflow approaching maximum utilization of the equipment and personnel.

The following development involves reference to several related charts. The rationale employed in developing the automated concept deals with the distribution of operation cycle times—cycle times that represent potential mechanized times. The central idea is to determine whether or not there is some predominating cycle time among all of the appropriate operations that could establish a basic cycle time design specification for the automated system. Fortunately, there is—as will be shown.

The operations portrayed in the operation flowchart, Figure 8–1, are listed in Table 8–1. The entries in Table 8–1 in the column headed "Machine Cycle Time" represent the nominal time that an automated machine would require to perform the operation. The values have been derived by forming the sum

TABLE 8-1
Cycle Time and Balancing Worksheet

Operation		Machine Cycle Time (seconds)	Automated Cycle Time (seconds)	Notes
No.	Description			
325	Finish set bands to collar	8	12	
340				Auxiliary operation
341	Trim collar	5	0	Not required (higher precision)
342	Top stitch collar	14	24	
343	Turn collar	9	12	
344	Line and run stitch	11	12	
345	Start set bands to collar	5	6	
360				Auxiliary operation
380				Auxiliary operation
381	Hem collar band	6	6	

of the sew, internal alignment, and transfer time for each operation. To keep on the main line of this presentation, the details in calculating the machine cycle time are not shown. It is sufficient to note that standard data were used and allowances were made for mechanization. The determination of the automated cycle time will be discussed shortly.

The frequency distribution of the machine cycle times for all operations is shown in Figure 8–2. A reading of this distribution shows that the single highest number of operations have a cycle time of 6 seconds. If three of the 7-second operations are placed with the 6-second group, that group would comprise 55 percent of all sewing operations. (From the hardware standpoint, adjustments up or down, where feasible, relate to machine design and speed control of the operating machinery.)

The next group of operations, from 7 seconds to 12 seconds, represent 31 percent of the operations placed in a 12-second

FIGURE 8–2
Distribution of Unadjusted Machine Cycle Times

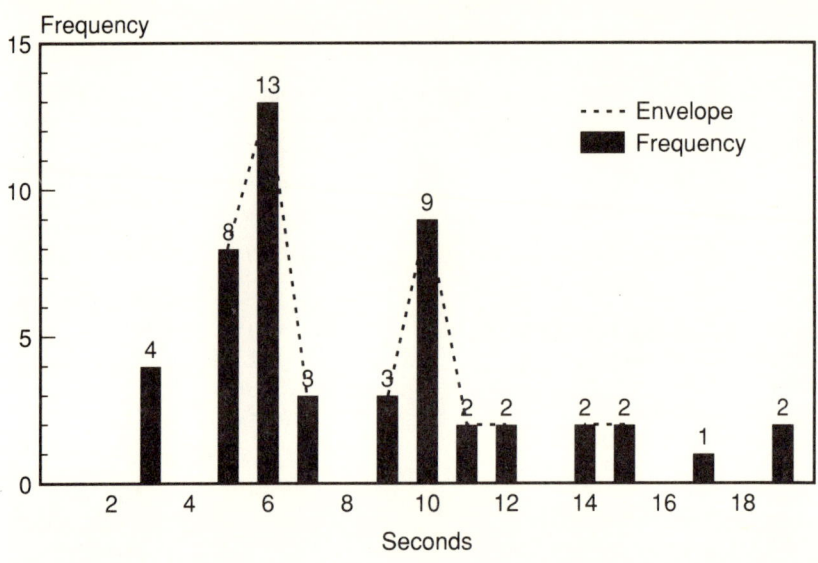

operation group. Both the 6- and 12-second group represent 86 percent of all operations. The balance would fall in a 24-second group. From this analysis, 6 seconds is seen as the basic cycle time for the automated system. It is this basic 6-second cycle time that is used to establish the automated cycle time shown in Table 8–1.

As is apparent in Table 8–1, the automated cycle times are obtained by adjusting the machine times up to the nearest 6-second multiple that would provide for line balancing of the automated system. Thus, operation number 325 with an 8-second cycle time is adjusted to a 12-second automated cycle time.

The question can be asked: What if the distribution of cycle times is flat across the frequency scale? There are alternatives. The first approach is to determine whether or not the work content (and therefore time) of each operation could be changed to facilitate the setting of a basic cycle time. Another alternative is to investigate the product design as it relates to operations and automation.

Having established the basic cycle time of 6 seconds for this product, the next step is to develop a schematic diagram of the automated system. This is shown in Figure 8–3. A key is provided for the symbolic notation. Several things are worth noting in the figure:

1. The system is balanced at a 6-second cycle time. For example, two production lines are provided for the 12-second operations.
2. The key shows symbolic notations for three classes of operations: automatic, semi-automatic, and manual. Automatic operations are technician monitored, semi-automatic operations are partially operator assisted, and manual operations are full operator/machine stations.
3. In the branches shown in the figure, all of the sew operations are judged automatable by current technology. (However, further downstream in the conceptual system some operations were seen as semiautomatic and some manual.)
4. A staffing assignment is determined by the level of automation class. Technicians are assigned to monitor five to seven automated stations. Semiautomated stations are assigned partial operator staffing. Manual operations are full time operator/machine stations.

System Reliability

At this point it might be well to discuss the subject of system reliability. As used here, the term *system reliability* refers to the percentage of time good production is taking place. By definition, a serially linked machine (station or operation) accepts the previously processed piece from the former machine, processes it, and then passes the part directly to the subsequent machine. In this kind of in-line system, it is apparent that a failure of any one of the serially linked stations to produce good work, because of process, mechanism, or material defect, causes the whole line to shut down. The term *system reliability* thus

146 Chapter 8

FIGURE 8-3
Schematic Diagram of Automated System

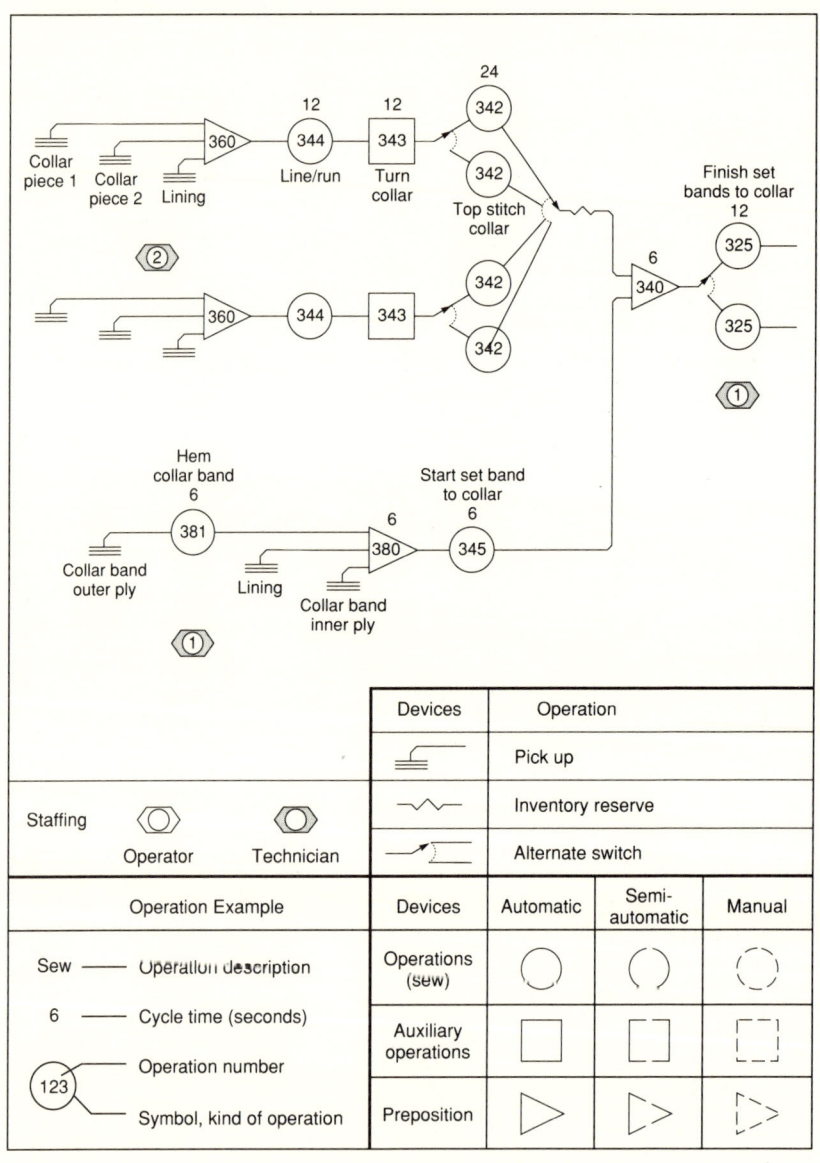

refers to the percentage of the time good production is coming off the end machine of the system considered.

As an example, consider a serial system consisting of five serially linked stations. Further, assume that the causes of failure at each station are mutually exclusive. As applied to this situation, the laws of probability state that serially linked stations with mutually exclusive failure causes would yield a net system reliability equal to the product of the respective reliabilities of each station.[6] Thus, if the reliabilities of five stations were as shown in the following expression, then the reliability of the system would be calculated as:

System reliability = .99 × .99 × .98 × .96 × .98 = 90%

There are at least two measures that can be taken to improve the reliability of serial systems. One is to include an inventory reserve as shown in the earlier diagrams. If the size of the inventory reserve is adjusted to equal the mean time to repair, and inventory reserves are replicated throughout the system, this could improve overall reliability. (A downstream line could momentarily fail while allowing its supply line to rebuild inventory that may have been depleted.)

Another method that can be employed to improve system reliability is to provide parallel stations for those with low reliability. Here again, simulation software can be useful in analyzing operating systems.

Production Rate
Continuing on with the development, recall the results of the analysis of the complete system yielded a basic 6-second cycle time for the automated system. At a system reliability of 75 percent, this would produce 450 shirts per hour:

(3600 seconds/hr.) × (.75) ÷ (6-second cycle) = 450 shirts/hour

For those interested in the specific application in the needle-trades industry, the results of the complete analysis yielded the figures shown in Table 8–2.

TABLE 8–2
Requirements, Manual/Automated System (Staffing and Equipment Requirements at a Production Rate of 450 Shirts per Hour)

	Manual System	Automated System
Staffing		
Operators	81	27
Technicians	2	23
Equipment		
Automated sewing machines	—	34
Semiautomated	—	17
Manual	87	19
Equipment Life		
	15 years	5 years

In the development, various concepts are presented. One can question each step of the development and change any one of the indices. But once the values and schemata are accepted, the rationale leads to the production rate of an automated system. This is a key step.

The determination of an automated production rate, as shown earlier, allows one to determine the equivalent staffing and equipment compliment that would be required to produce at the same rate with a present manual process. The labor and capital equipment recovery cost of the manual process can be evaluated in dollar figures. Judgments (based upon similar systems) can be made about staffing for the automated system. Similarly, staffing numbers can be evaluated in dollar figures for the automated system. Thus we would have:

Manual Process	Automated System
Staffing $ (known)	Staffing $ (estimated)
Equipment recovery $ (known)	Equipment recovery $ (unknown)

Present Worth

Using present worth (PW) analysis, the relationship can be employed:

PW_p present process = PW_a automated system

PW_p (Staff \$ + Equipment \$) = PW_a (Staff \$ + Equipment ?)

This relationship can be solved for the limiting capital equipment value (cost) of the automated system. This represents the second key step in the rationale. An index on the first cost of the automated system is useful in evaluating the potential development.

At this stage, application of the general methodology is apparent. The specific dollar values will depend upon the specifics of the application. Subsequent questions would focus on the feasibility of designing and building the components of the conceptual automated system. In addition to the equipment, an automated system would require greatly expanded services and utilities, which would have to be factored into the analysis.

In employing present worth comparison of alternative operations with different equipment lives, the least common multiple of the different lives of the facilities must be used in the computation.[7] In the illustration presented, the life of the sewing machine is taken at 15 years. The life of the automated sewing system is taken at 5 years. Thus, the common on multiple life for the study's purposes is 15 years in a present worth computation.

HARDWARE SEWING AUTOMATION

The previous development has dealt with conceptual automation. For the interested reader, the following paragraphs deal with the subject of actual automated sewing. How is it accomplished? Here again, as mentioned in earlier chapters, the focus must be on the material and process.

Those who have joined two pieces of cloth with a sewing machine realize that the presser foot has to come down and hold a section of the material while the needle plunges through the fabric in making the stitch. When the needle is retracted, the material can be moved. The key to an actual patented[8] mechanism on automated sewing is based on the use of a flexible coupling between a fabric drive plate and the fabric. While the drive is continuous, the presser foot clamps the material when the needle plunges through the material. When the presser foot is released, the flexible coupling moves the material incrementally to each new position in the path. The fact that fabric is flexible also aids the process.

In addition to automating the actual sewing operation, the feasibility of picking up one single piece part of fabric from a stack has been proven. Three alternate ways of accomplishing this include a venturi plate, adhesive surface, and mechanical sharp-point pickup.

This process of automation is, of course, unending. While for some products the marketing adline of "hand-made" sells, most of us couldn't afford an automobile if it was hand-made! *Automation is not the whole key to productivity, but where appropriate, it can be effective in improving quality and reducing cost.*

CHAPTER SUMMARY

In undertaking an automation project there are several preliminary considerations:

1. Is the design of the part stable, and what is the expected life?
2. What is the annual planning level and the demand throughout the year?
3. Should the part be redesigned to facilitate automated fabrication?
4. What are the expected difficult parts of the project?
5. Does economic analysis indicate an attractive return on investment?

6. Is this a candidate for a fixed (hard), versus flexible, manufacturing scheme?

To reduce the risk in a major development, it is generally advisable to commit an initial prove-out investment of up to about 10 percent of the expected total project cost. The initial step is to identify the most difficult part of the process or concept, then test it and prove it is feasible.

In planning for the automation of some function or process, it is essential to understand and know the full characteristics of the inputs to the machine or system.

As in all developments that are going to involve people, the manner in which human interaction is conducted and dealt with has a considerable bearing on the success of the venture. Friendly businesslike relationships with people in the shop should be maintained regardless of changes in the technology.

A rationale is presented for developing an automated system concept of a manual manufacturing process. The procedure determines a basic cycle time for the automated system and, therefore, the production rate. From this, the equivalent staffing and equipment requirements for the manual system can be determined. Staffing for the automated system can be assigned. Using present worth analysis, the systems can be compared, solving for a limiting present worth of the capital equipment of the automated system.

In the course of the material, the subjects of line balancing and system reliability are discussed. Notes on actual automation in the needle-trades industry are presented.

CHAPTER 9

MANAGEMENT, TOOLS AND TECHNOLOGY

CHANGES IN MANUFACTURING TECHNOLOGY

Changes in manufacturing technology that are taking place will have an effect on the practice of management. Classical modes in a rigid structure are giving way to a different kind of involvement in the manufacturing culture. One technological reason is that computer networking will affect the structure of organizations and the conduct of work.[1] In the drive to increase productivity and quality, another factor to consider is that managers and supervisors are delegating a larger share of responsibility for initiating changes and corrective action when necessary in the manufacturing process. Further, some manufacturing systems make self-direction evident. For management, factors like these involve increasing access to appropriate information and forgoing certain prerogatives that were previously reserved.

As is the case in the practice of management, the need for generally recognized skills and qualifications continues. There may be, however, somewhat of a paradigm shift in the context. The rate of change of both global competition and technology suggests the increased need for an adaptive/reactive capability. The books *Mastering Change*[2] and *The Technology Connection, Strategy and Change in the Information Age*[3] address the issue and context. Prerequisites in coping with the change certainly involve a good semantic orientation, a capability in differentiation, and an understanding of dynamic, statistical, and nonlinear systems.

FIGURE 9-1
Development Considerations for Management

Management (general)
- Invest in long-range goals over excess current profits.
- Support the broad practice of quality control (TQC).
- Invest in manufacturing development programs.

Sales
- Provide close attention and response to the needs of the customer.

Engineering Design and Research
- Provide investment in research and capitalize on developments.
- Design for quality product and manufacture.
- Shorten the product design to manufacturing engineering phase.

Industrial/Manufacturing Engineering
- Provide for increased planning and support to manufacturing.
- Pursue improved processes and workflow in the plant.
- Eliminate or reduce setup time (tool design and shop).
- Initiate continuous and effective pursuit of cost reduction.

Manufacturing
- Create a climate where supervisors encourage workers to make suggestions and initiate corrective action.
- Support and maintain continuous quality control practices.
- Material Control: Develop the most appropriate inventory and production control system. Evaluate application of JIT.
- Purchasing: Assure qualifications of vendors as part of cycle.
- Maintenance: Develop preventive maintenance program.
- Consider alternate incentive system over piecework.

The current period may be perceived as a period of extensive manufacturing development. If the current trend exhibited by some of the leading industries continues, industrial historians may regard this as a period of considerable change in many ways. A list of development considerations for management in seeking higher productivity and product quality is shown in Figure 9-1.

The appropriateness of each potential development application under consideration must be evaluated in the context of the specific manufacturing plant. For example, it is possible to have an effective system in which you may not see any computers in the production line.[4] On the other end of the spectrum, a computerized NC lathe can machine a part while the operation is monitored using a constant stream of quality control data on a computer monitor. This, of course, provides instant information on whether the part is good. Both situations can be productive.

As a qualifying note, on at least one of the newer technologies receiving much current attention (the inventory pull system involving JIT/kanbans) there are valid reasons why it may not be appropriate for some industries. Some of these reasons relate to low-volume, nonrepetitive manufacture, or a situation in which variations in processes and options cannot be known in advance.[5] In these cases, management is well advised to evaluate the applications carefully.

At appropriate places in previous chapters, various analytical techniques and tools have been employed to analyze and solve problems. The techniques presented should not be interpreted to imply that a tool or technique is the thing that gets the job done—in a vacuum, so to speak. It's OK to talk about tools and technology, but *managers tuned to the current operating climate put people first*. Donald Peterson looked for the manager who developed a good working relationship with the operators in his shop.[6] When good relationships are evident, it's a tipoff that people feel comfortable, consulted, and part of the team. And, it's how good ideas can come from the person doing the job.

MANAGEMENT CHARTS

The following section presents some of the more useful graphical techniques that can be employed in analysis, management, and control. The charts are presented in three groups. While commonly employed charts are shown in each group, the placement of charts in groups is a convenience in presentation. Any chart is applicable to any field. The first set of charts is shown in Figure 9–2. The use and construction of each chart is explained. For the nontechnical person, the usefulness is apparent. For the engineer, the details are convenient, but all are encouraged to refer to texts on the subjects. The moving annual

FIGURE 9–2
Management Charts

Moving Annual Total

Use: Provide meaningful index of the level of conformance to any stated annual goal.

Construction:
- Start with annual total.
- Add each new month value.
- Subtract corresponding aged monthly figure.

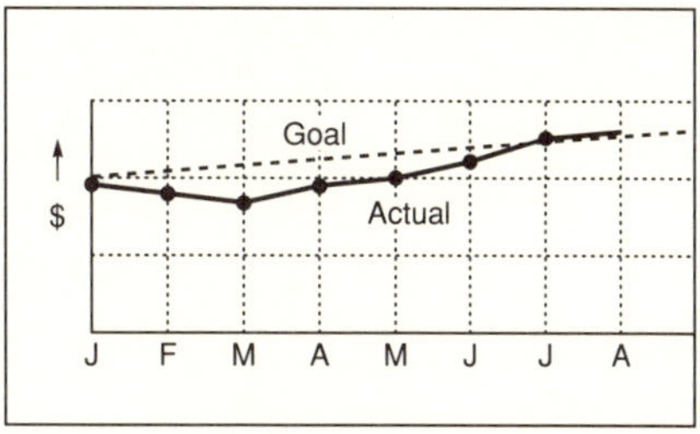

[Chart: $ vs months J F M A M J J A, showing Goal (dashed) and Actual lines]

Variances

Use: Principle of exception, allows you to follow up on variation against standard.

Construction:
- Establish standard.
- Record actual.
- Calculate variation.

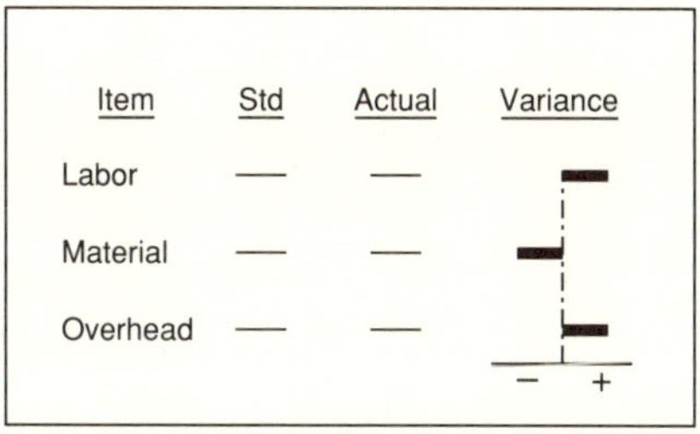

Item	Std	Actual	Variance
Labor	—	—	
Material	—	—	
Overhead	—	—	

− +

Project Schedule

Use: To help manage projects.

Construction:
- Determine tasks, staffing, and costs against a time schedule.

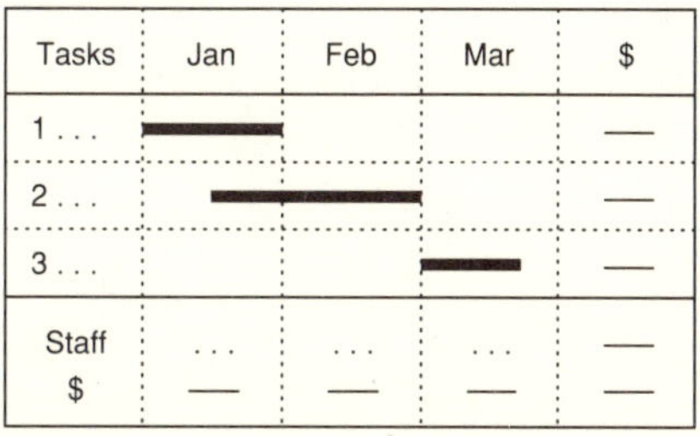

Tasks	Jan	Feb	Mar	$
1...	▬▬▬			—
2...		▬▬▬		—
3...			▬▬	—
Staff $	...	...	...	—

---

total (MAT) chart shown in Figure 9–2 has several properties. It:

- Provides an annualized picture of the change of variable charted.
- Permits performance to be compared against a goal.

- Disposes of seasonal fluctuation problems in interpreting monthly data.

The MAT chart, along with monthly data, is useful in indicating steps that should be undertaken to meet annual goals.

For comparisons employing standard cost systems, it is common to tabulate actual cost compared with the standard and note the variance. The format is illustrated in the variance chart shown in Figure 9–2. Follow-up action can be undertaken to determine the cause of excessive variation so as to correct and/or reconcile the situation.

Major projects warrant preparation of a project schedule. A capsule illustration is presented in Figure 9–2. The schedule provides a plan for the sequence of tasks, personnel, and dollar requirements. A more elaborate PERT (program evaluation and review technique) chart (not shown here) is employed to reveal the critical path. The critical path represents the sequential trail that controls the total time span of the project.

Several charts that are employed in industrial and manufacturing engineering are shown in Figure 9–3. A common need exists to determine the relationship between two variables. For example, one may wish to know the correlation between investment in training and production quality; or, the relationship between investment in preventive maintenance and productivity. While information about a relationship shown in a scatter diagram is useful, care should be exercised in the selection of variables. Even though an X variable and a Y variable move together, it does not *necessarily* indicate that an increase in the X variable *causes* the Y variable to increase or decrease.

It is not uncommon for those in business and industry to have more to do than they can reasonably be expected to accomplish within the time and cost restraints. The Pareto chart, shown in Figure 9–3, is useful in portraying the tasks on which to focus—those with greatest return, dollar value, or urgency. If the data from an analysis of machine failures is organized in a Pareto curve, it presents a clear indication of primary problems

FIGURE 9–3
Industrial/Manufacturing Engineering Charts

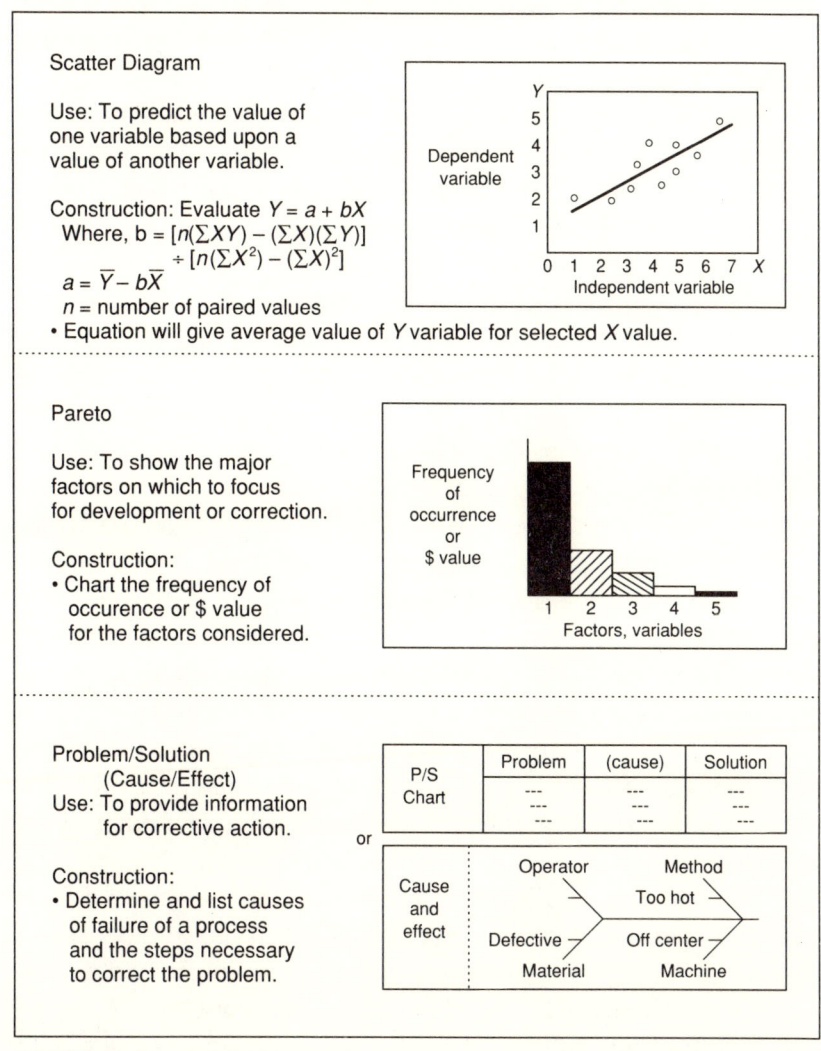

to address. The time and cost to repair may also be factors bearing on the priorities.

When a comprehensive analysis has been made of causes of machine or process failure, the information can be formatted for easy reference and servicing. The form is shown in problem/ solution or cause/effect diagrams. In addition, shop operators, maintenance, and manufacturing engineers should investigate to determine which of the problems can be eliminated by upgrading or development work.

Several leading charts that are employed in quality control are shown in Figure 9–4. Fundamental to the basis of quality control is the use of (control) relationships that are based upon statistical (random) variation in processes in which there are no assignable causes. The general objective is to provide an operation or process in which the distribution of output falls within the specification of the property (e.g., dimension, hardness, or other variable). The second objective is to control the process so that the distribution is reasonably centered and the range does not exceed the specification.

The histogram shown in Figure 9–4 shows the generalized pattern. The $\bar{x}$, R charts show the graphical tools used to control variables. When the sampled points fall beyond the control limits (shown with a dotted line) for either average or range, it is an indication that something may have happened with the system of causes. The process should then be checked and brought back into regulation.

The P chart is employed to control processes in which the part is either satisfactory or unsatisfactory. The chart provides a record of the percent defective for an attribute of a part. As an example, the tank leaks or does not leak.

The use and application of these charts is enhanced by a foundation in statistics. The graphical illustrations and construction notes present the general concepts. The interested reader can pursue the specific details of his or her concern.

It should be clear that the presentation of all of the charts and graphs does not imply or stand for the fundamental management process. These and other graphs merely portray some of the cost and value relationships that management can employ in improving productivity and product quality. Managers' skill lies in their leadership in obtaining their companies' goals.

FIGURE 9–4
Quality Control Charts

Histogram (Frequency Distribution)

Use: To display the profile, showing the most frequent value and the range from the given data.

Construction:
- Select scale of values for horizontal axis.
- Use vertical scale for frequency.
- Plot distribution of data.

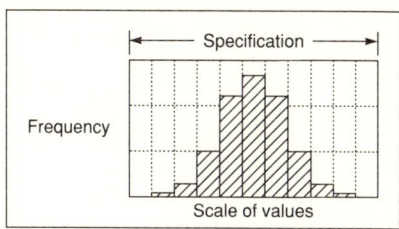

$\bar{X}$, R Chart

Use: Control and correct process.
- $\bar{X}$ chart shows the collective trend about the mean or norm.
- R chart shows the extent of the variation between (group) items.

Construction:
- Select sample size (commonly 5).
- Calculate and plot average ($\bar{X}$) and the range of values (R).
- Calculate grand average $\bar{\bar{x}}$ and average range ($\bar{R}$).
- Upper and lower control limits = $\bar{\bar{x}} \pm A_2\bar{R}$, ($A_2 = 0.577$ for sample size 5).
- Upper control limit for range = $D_4\bar{R}$, ($D_4 = 2.114$ for sample size 5).

P Chart

Use: Control chart for attributes that monitors percent defective.

Construction:
- Select a number of subgroups (usually 20), each containing n units selected in sequence and inspected for attributes.
- Calculate the average percent defective ($\bar{P}$).
- Upper control limit, UCL = $\bar{P} + 3\sqrt{[\bar{P}(1 - \bar{P})/n]}$.

USEFUL CONCEPTS AND GRAPHICAL TOOLS

Product Life Cycles

There are, of course, many other concepts and graphical tools that are useful. In planning for long-range needs, the concept and consideration of product life cycles is important. An understanding of shifts in market demand and the need for new product lines provides for continued profitability.

Learning Curve

Use of the learning curve is helpful in estimating labor costs, but more significantly, its use has been integrated into the business strategies of companies.[7] The application is based upon the concept (from statistical studies) that during the learning period, the average operational labor hours per unit decrease by a fixed fraction as the cumulative output doubles.[8] A rate reduction of 20 percent, for example, is called an 80-percent learning curve. Thus, if one completed an initial lot of 20 units, for which the average labor time per unit was 30 hours, then an order that would double the cumulative, in this case 20 units, would require an average unit time of 30 times 80 percent, or 24 hours. The relationship is as follows:

Quantities/Lot	Cumulative Quantities	Average Time/Unit
20	20	30
20	40	24 (30 × 0.80)
40	80	19.2 (24 × 0.80)

Travel Chart

A relationship often employed in plant layout is the travel chart. This is not unlike the common distance chart on a road map. In laying out operations and departments in manufacturing, one of the goals is to reduce materials handling. Moving a part or assembly from one place to another adds nothing to its intrinsic value. Minimizing the required moves of parts and assemblies reduces manufacturing cost.

Matrix

There are many uses for a common matrix, which provides a coordinate cell value or relationship for associated rows and columns. Computer spread-sheet programs are good examples of matrix relationships. Some organizations prepare a matrix of outstanding proposals with the associated probability of obtaining each contract as a means of estimating the net expected dollar value of business.

Earlier chapters have illustrated various development applications. Many improvements in manufacturing operations can be introduced with little or no investment. If the better method can be readily demonstrated, it can be instituted promptly, providing it does not have a negative effect on the function, performance, and appeal of the product.

Economic Analysis

For development applications that involve consideration of new machine tools or equipment, assets that are capitalized, an economic analysis is ordinarily prepared. The use of the net present value (NPV)[9] can be employed. The NPV is the sum of the cash inflows discounted at a rate equal to the company's cost of capital minus the cost of the initial investment in the project. If the NPV is equal to or greater than zero, the firm will earn a return equal to or greater than its required return or cost of capital.

Computer Programs and Simulations

With the state of computer and software technology, the analysis and solutions to many needs and problems are readily available. The applications can be in the form of solutions to discrete one-time inquiries or problems, or to dynamic simulations in which variables are changed to explore various options in working out a solution.

The capabilities provide quick response for engineers and managers needing solutions to business problems. The program STORM,[10] for example, presents 16 modules on the main menu. Included are modules on:

- Statistical process control.
- Inventory management.
- Assembly-line balancing.
- Production scheduling.
- Forecasting.

The software program also presents 11 other modules.

There are many problems and projects in which it would be helpful to simulate the production situation. What will happen, from the model standpoint, to the through-put if we install a conveyor here with two additional machines? What will the effect be if we . . . ? Computer simulations can deal with aspects such as mean time between failure and mean time to repair. While the human interaction is always a concern, the capability of uncovering "structural" problems in a system before the installation is helpful.

The dynamic factory simulation program FlexWork[11] provides a deterministic model—that is, one that does not contain random elements, but rather in which the future course of the system is determined by its state at the present (and/or in the past). The program simulates several concepts in manufacturing, including:

- The dynamics of introducing a new product.
- The "hair-trigger" feel of a JIT factory.
- Resource-constrained work scheduling.

The program provides an interactive debugger for exploring and working out adjustments to the system.

Another simulation program for manufacturing and material distribution is AUTOMOD.[12] The program runs on an IBM 386 PC and the Macintosh II family of products. It provides three-dimensional animated graphics.

Preventive maintenance, as mentioned in an earlier chapter, is an industrial practice that supports productivity goals. The software program TMS,[13] Total Maintenance System, addresses the various tasks in a preventive maintenance program.

Programs like these and others can be effective in improving productivity and quality. The tools and technology are available where needed. But it should be understood that much can be learned about what to do and how to make it work by listening to the people in the ranks, who may already know what to do. This is called "people empowerment."

Malcolm Baldrige National Quality Award

One of the seven criteria in evaluating candidates for the Malcolm Baldrige National Quality Award is *"Leadership: The Senior Executives' Success in Creating and Sustaining a Quality Culture."*[14] This statement underscores the reality that top management must have a sufficient understanding of and a substantial commitment to a quality program.

People in manufacturing, by observing the consistency of support on actions involving product quality, come to know about management commitment. Positive commitment reinforces their actions in producing quality products!

Most of the concepts and development programs are interrelated. For example, if you do not have good quality control, an abrupt reduction of inventory could be disastrous. In reducing inventory lot size, any defects in parts will be detected more quickly in subsequent operations, allowing for corrective feedback. If you have good quality control and JIT, investment in inventory can be reduced.

CONCERNS OF MANAGEMENT

What then should be the uppermost concerns of management? Well, there are several. In the course of current operations, those seeking to increase productivity and product quality should do the following:

Customer:
- Seek to determine and provide the product features sought by your customers. These include good design features, pricing, and delivery.

Product:
- Shorten the development time from product conception to production.
- Provide good communication and teamwork with which you can telescope the normal sequential tasks of design, manufacturing engineering, and tooling.

Manufacturing:
- Establish and maintain companywide quality control.
- Seek the potential of your people to contribute to improvements. This is called "employee empowerment."
- Develop effective work cells and **JIT** inventory systems where appropriate.
- Provide industrial and manufacturing engineering support to facilitate production planning, reduction of setup time, and cost reduction.

CHAPTER SUMMARY

New technology and the drive for productivity and quality are changing the context of management. Employee empowerment is becoming recognized as a potential untapped source of improvement. Management is presented with numerous considerations for development that ranges from product design to manufacturing operations.

There are many tools and techniques available to management and engineers for analyzing and solving business problems. The tools are applicable for management, engineering, and shop applications in quality control.

In addition to manual methods, there are numerous computer programs that can be employed to analyze or solve business problems. Simulation software facilitates the study and analysis of a production situation as an aid to uncovering potential problems before an actual installation and helps to assure an optimum "structural" solution.

Those seeking to increase productivity and product quality should address the needs of the customer, shorten the development time from product conception to production, and undertake development programs in manufacturing, including total quality control, effective inventory and production control, and related manufacturing engineering applications.

APPENDIX A

OPERATIONAL AUDIT

It is customary for most companies (and a requirement for those publicly held) to have an annual financial audit to assure conformance to generally accepted accounting principles. The concept of utilizing audits to assess the operational aspects of engineering and manufacturing is equally valid. It provides a means of checking, and thus regulating, control against standards and objectives.

Regardless of the scope and frequency of the audit, the task is like obtaining feedback on performance. How are we doing? One way of viewing the activity symbolically is much like an analog of a closed-loop feedback system illustrated in Figure A–1. In the simplified block diagram of the system, input is provided that specifies the desired output. During operation, adjustments are made by the control system until the difference between the desired and actual output is as small as required. In operation, the output is sensed and fed back in a manner so as to reduce the difference between the objective and actual output. But this, of course, is similar to checking the progress of work or auditing an operation.

The analogy can be carried one step further. In closed-loop control systems, the term *transient response* defines the response of the output with respect to time when input is suddenly changed. An illustration of this is shown in Figure A–2. Though there are limitations in making the analogy, the diagrams can serve as useful mental images—reminders of the constant need for feedback in a manner and time so as to be able to meet operating objectives throughout changes in the economy, technology, and market.

Closely related to the subject of audits are the terms *system analysis* and *performance appraisals*. The distinctions are largely a matter of scope and timing or frequency of the process. Today's needs require quick reaction and prompt feedback on performance.

There is a caveat on the timing and character of performance appraisal of personnel. In his writings, W. Edwards Deming mentions

FIGURE A–1
Closed-Loop Feedback System

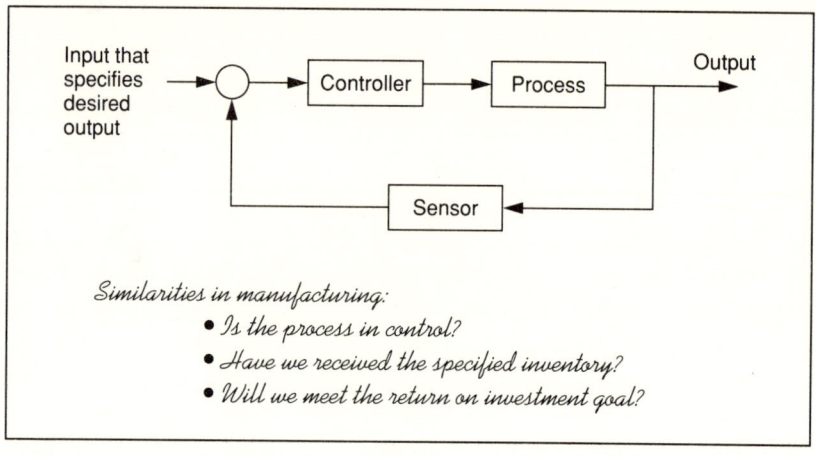

Similarities in manufacturing:
- *Is the process in control?*
- *Have we received the specified inventory?*
- *Will we meet the return on investment goal?*

FIGURE A–2
Transient Response of System

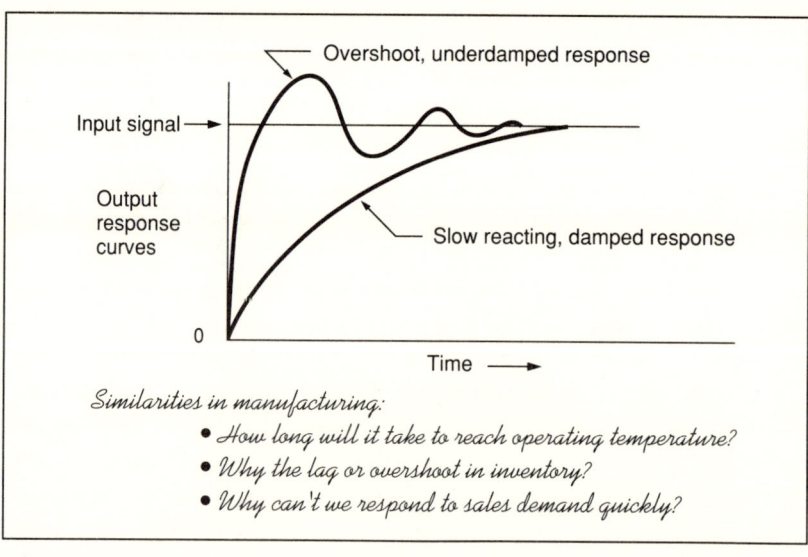

Similarities in manufacturing:
- *How long will it take to reach operating temperature?*
- *Why the lag or overshoot in inventory?*
- *Why can't we respond to sales demand quickly?*

the negative effects on people's feelings, and he notes the short-range-goal focus of once-a-year MBO (management by objectives). Who can argue against goals? However, the evaluation of people's performance should be conducted in a timely, supportive manner (daily or as required), and managers should be empowered to advance reasonable long-range goals along with meeting current needs. This discussion qualifies the approach to audits, system analysis, and performance appraisal. System analysis and audits document what is going on and seek to uncover areas for improvement.

Prior to embarking on a new development program, an analysis or audit of the existing system is often indicated. Companies that utilize external services are seeking objectivity and the opportunity to uncover new potential areas for development. Corporations typically use semi-independent staff consultants for divisional audits.

The scope of the analysis (and development) can be as broad or narrow as appropriate, with two qualifications. First, the analysis (and performance) of a single business function cannot properly be made without examining the quality and character of the input to that function and the context (constraints of the larger system). Second, the suitability of the output to associated functions should be determined. A case in point: While a material control department trying just-in-time may be meritorious, it is not likely to succeed without a host of other context factors like effective quality control, just to mention one.

The approach to an audit may range from a primarily *results-oriented* to a more *structured* analysis covering the many aspects of operations. In a results-oriented audit, the analysis would have a focus as shown in Figure A–3. It can be argued that the prime requirement, after all, is getting results on factors that affect profitability and return on investment! True. But only looking at a snapshot of a current year's profitability does not provide all the information necessary to evaluate the results in relation either to current development underway or to long-range strategy that will favorably affect future years. An understanding of the strategy is also important.

In a highly structured audit, the work-order processing system from order entry to billing may be studied. If information on the systems and procedures does not exist or is out of date, a comprehensive documentation may be prepared. This is the first step in attempting to gain an understanding of the existing system.

FIGURE A–3
Focus of Results-Oriented Audit

Research: How many discoveries, inventions and patents were produced?
Engineering: How many new products were designed this year?
Engineering and manufacturing engineering: Has the design-to-manufacturing cycle been reduced? How much?
Manufacturing engineering: What was the improvement in productivity and cost reduction?
Quality control: What is the rate of product returns, rework, and scrap?
Material control: Has inventory cost been reduced without stock-outs?
Labor standards: Are work standards in-line? What about labor variation?
Supervision and personnel: What is the record on training and supervision?
Equipment: What new equipment was installed? What is the percentage of machine utilization?

Figure A–4 shows an example of documentation of a plant system. One advantage of the format is that it provides a clear audit trail, showing the actions, documents, and departmental function involved.

In the course of reviewing the system, numerous questions can be raised. It is common to find that some task being performed involves the preparation of a report that no one reads or needs and that finally ends up in a storage file. The major values of documenting the system and procedures include:

1. It provides an opportunity to uncover and eliminate obsolete and/or unnecessary procedures.
2. It provides the basis for introducing improvements in the system (manual or computer) that can be checked against the existing needs and control.
3. It serves as an excellent security and training document for new personnel.

Following the preparation of one of these system documentations, the newly hired controller reported that the material saved him three months' learning time in his new job!

A comprehensive structured audit program consists of several major steps:

1. System study, analysis, and data collection.

2. Evaluation and synthesis leading to a report.
3. Presentation, discussion, and action on recommendations.
4. Follow-up on upgrading operations.

The program may include analysis of:

Organizational structure, objectives, and policies:

- Consideration of organizational structure in relation to general objectives, strategies, and operating needs.
- A review of policies—are plant policies understood, observed, and consistent with current operations?

General management reporting and control system:

- An examination of management's reporting and control methods for adequacy, including preparation of periodic reports, scheduled management meetings, and related control procedures.

Personnel and staffing:

- Are personnel qualifications and staffing adequate for the organization?

Sales and marketing program:

- Does a strong sales and marketing program exist?

Product/service line:

- Scope and character of the product/service lines—the degree of technical complexity will determine the criteria in evaluating the adequacy of the organization's structure, systems, and specific departmental operations.

Plant systems and procedures:

- An analysis of the operating system cycle through sales, engineering, production, and accounting—is the design of the system sound? Are there any special problems in order processing, timing, communications, and control?

General plant layout:

FIGURE A–4   Documentation, Plant Systems, and Procedures

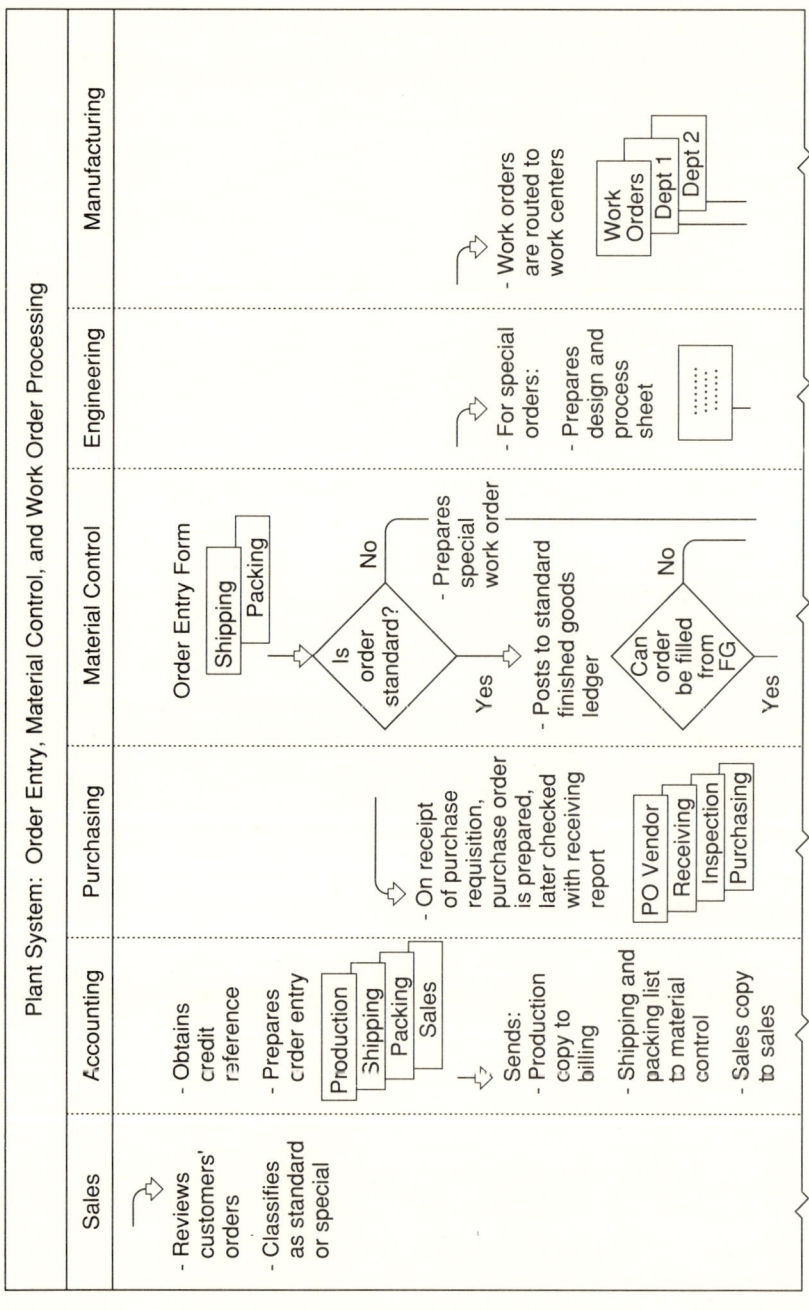

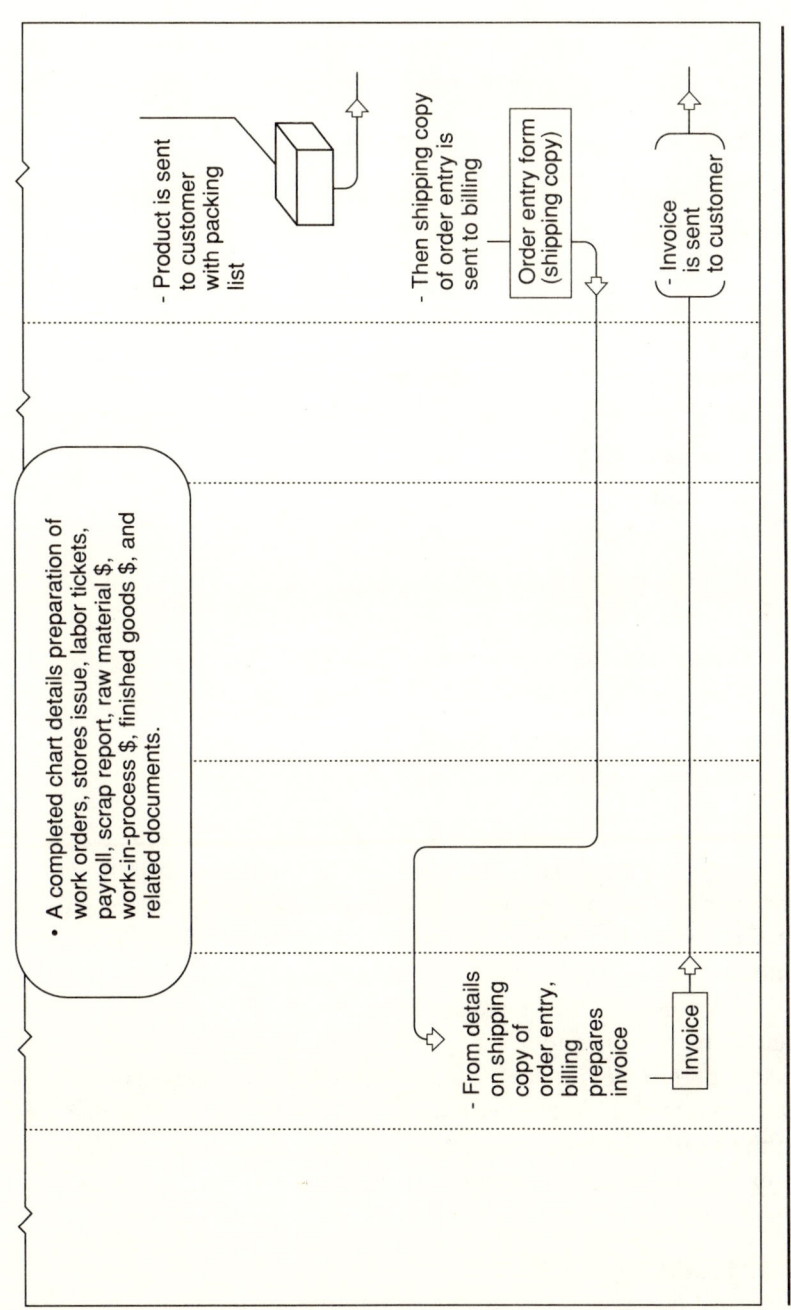

- Does the overall manufacturing layout provide for good workflow, operating effectiveness, and safety of personnel?

Physical facilities and equipment:

- Do physical facilities and equipment meet good current standards?

General and departmental effectiveness (analysis in the following areas):

- Management, responsibility and authority
- Productivity
- Quality control
- Cost control
- Labor and machine utilization
- Preventive maintenance
- Personnel training
- Operating and plant safety
- Standards
- Evaluation of operating ratios
- Planning function, current and long range

In the course of a comprehensive analysis, areas are usually uncovered in which operating problems can be resolved and/or potential improvements advanced. The report to management will provide an opportunity to review and act on the recommendations for development.

A consultant can be engaged to conduct audit programs, or self-assessment can be undertaken. Those who have gone through the process of competing for the Malcolm Baldrige National Quality Award report obtaining numerous values in the course of the analysis and thought-provoking procedures. The core values and concepts of the examination for the quality award are embodied in seven categories:

1. Leadership
2. Information and analysis
3. Strategic quality planning
4. Human resource development and management

FIGURE A–5
Baldrige Award Criteria Framework

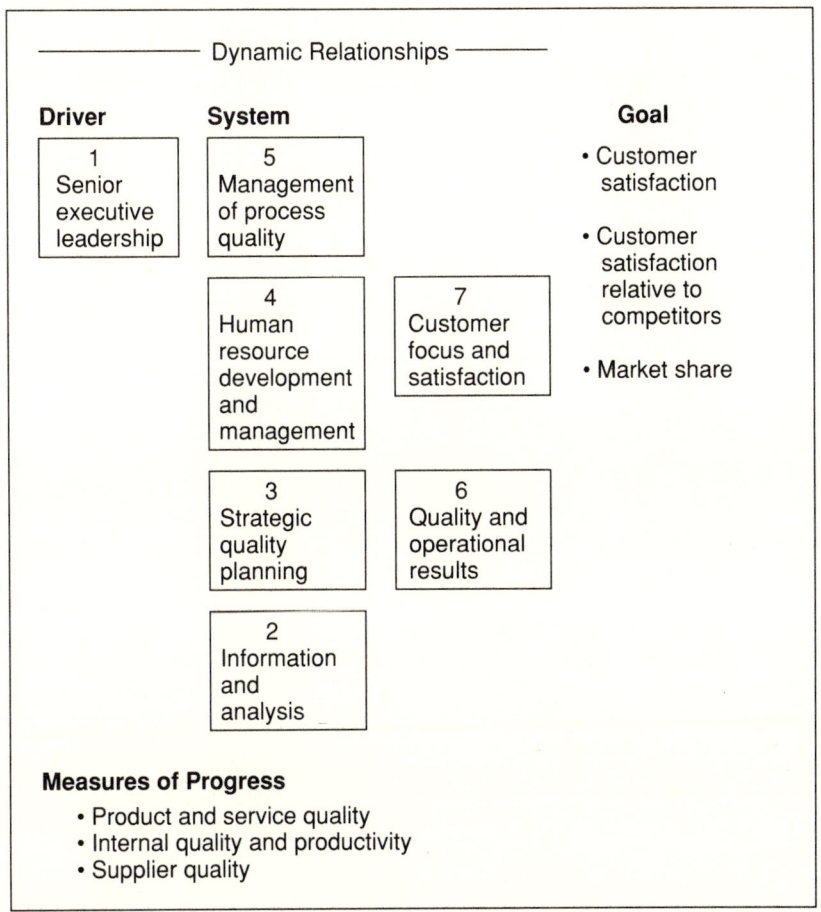

Source: Diagram in the 1992 Award Criteria, Malcolm Baldrige National Quality Award brochure, used with permission and slightly modified.

5. Management of process quality
6. Quality and operational results
7. Customer focus and satisfaction

The dynamic relationships between all elements of the system are recognized in the Baldrige Award Framework. The concept is shown in Figure A–5, based on the diagram on page 5 of the 1992 "Award

Criteria" brochure. It is significant to note that senior executive leadership is designated as the driver of the system. A company's senior leaders must create clear and visible personal commitment and involvement in the program. The benefits of an effective quality program are returned in the form of improved productivity and profitability.

APPENDIX B

QUALITY CONTROL CHART

The narrative program in Chapter 3 details the process for making a machine capability analysis. As explained, the purpose of a machine capability study is to determine whether or not the machine is capable of producing output within the specification. By comparison, the (nominal) objective of quality control is to maintain production within specification. (One should also not lose sight of the fact that effective quality control reduces cost.) While the actual charting of the average and range of values for variables is only one aspect of an effective quality control program, it is, nevertheless, the commonly accepted method of determining that a process is in statistical control.

This section amplifies the format of quality control charts for variables shown in Chapter 9 by providing a detailed example with actual data. The $\bar{x}$ (x-bar), R chart for variables is shown in Figure B–1. The chart presents the general relationships employed for the calculation of the upper control limit ($UCL\bar{X}$) and the lower control limit ($LCL\bar{X}$) for the average value of x, using a sample size of five pieces. The calculation of the control limit for range (CLR) is also shown.

The significance of the control limits, shown as dashed lines, is that no corrective action is indicated for the process as long as the average and range of each sample randomly fall within the limits. Even so, additional indications can be detected from certain patterns within control limits. To explore the subject further, the reader is encouraged to pursue the subject in Grant and Leavenworth's *Statistical Quality Control* or one of the many other references on the subject.

The chart is constructed as follows:

1. For an established and stable process, select a sample (five pieces in our case) of parts at some appropriate frequency, like each hour, more or less, according to the situation.
2. Compute the average and the range of each sample.
3. Continue the sampling for 10 or more sample sets of the process. In the example, 15 sample sets were taken of which 5 are shown.

Appendix B

FIGURE B–1
Control Chart for Variables

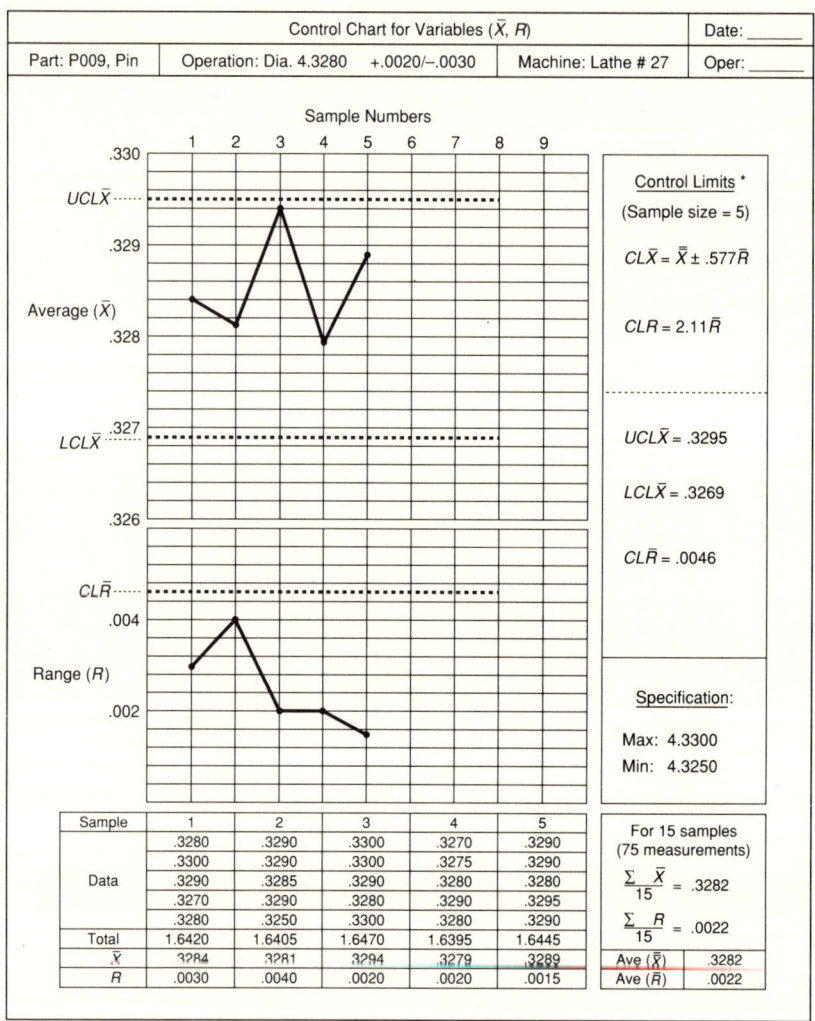

* The general relationships are based upon the original work of Walter A. Shewhart, since republished by the American Society of Quality Control. The values of the constants for different sample sizes can be found in the manual of the American Society for Testing and Materials.

Institute of Industrial Engineers

® *Supporting Systems Integrators*

The Institute of Industrial Engineers (IIE) is a non-profit international professional society of nearly 35,000 members whose principal endeavor is productivity and quality improvement through systems integration. IIE supports its members through a number of professional seminars and conferences, a variety of publications, and an ongoing public awareness program.

To receive more information about the benefits of becoming an IIE member (substantial discounts on seminar/conference registrations, books, magazines and other media, plus much more), simply complete the adjacent form and drop this card in the mail.

NAME

TITLE

COMPANY NAME

ADDRESS

CITY, STATE, ZIP

PHONE NUMBER

BRCAM-1

BUSINESS REPLY MAIL
First-class   Permit no. 49   Norcross, GA
POSTAGE WILL BE PAID BY ADDRESSEE

INSTITUTE OF INDUSTRIAL ENGINEERS
Customer Service Department
25 Technology Park
Norcross, GA 30092-9708

No Postage
Necessary
If Mailed
In The
United States

4. Calculate the grand average ($\bar{\bar{x}}$) and the average range ($\bar{R}$) as shown.
5. Compute the control limits (upper and lower) for the average values and the control limit for the range from the relationships given in Figure B–1.
6. To monitor the process, periodically select samples for the process and plot the computed values to check on the existence of statistical control.
7. A deviation of points beyond the control limits is a sign of an impending shift in the process. The system of (assignable) causes may have changed. Such changes may have been in the machine, tool, material, environment, method, or operator control.

The example shown is viewed as a useful tool in dealing with critical processes that warrant close control. The presence of good quality control is, however, more than just charting critical variables. The quality-conscious attitude and commitment of all people in the organization should be apparent and practiced for effective quality control.

APPENDIX C

ENGINEERING ECONOMIC ANALYSIS

The major decisions on investments that are capitalized—that are not expensed or charged off within a year—will normally involve an engineering economic analysis. Choices may exist between two or more alternatives. And, of course, choices also exist between the alternatives of replacing a machine in some given year or not replacing it—that is, doing nothing regarding the piece of equipment. Action on these economic choices, whether recognized or not, has an effect on both productivity and product quality.

A distinction should be made between an engineering economic analysis of a potential acquisition, in which its useful life is considered, and the accounting capitalization of an acquisition involving the annual charge for depreciation. The focus of an engineering economic analysis is to determine the best choice from among alternative (investment) projects. The actual accounting capitalization treatment of the annual depreciation charge in more recent years is controlled by IRS regulations as an instrument of fiscal policy. To illustrate the distinction, if a machine that has been given a 15-year accounting life is not productive after 5 years, the economic move would more likely be to replace it. That action (a write-off) will affect profitability in that year; but more importantly, if a better machine is installed, the productivity would be increased in the long run.

The common factors of an economic analysis are shown in Figure C–1. The entries list the basic factors that are considered.

At this point, with a calculated net savings per year, some persons calculate the payback period by dividing the initial investment by the net savings per year. The payback period method, although simple, does not really measure the merits of the investment but only the speed with which the investment cost might be recovered. Both the payback period and the inverse, the rate-of-return, ignore the *time value of cash flows*.

FIGURE C–1
Factors in Economic Analysis

	Present	Proposed
Basic factors		
First cost (installed cost)	—	XXX
Life	X	X
Present salvage value	XX	—
Resale value at end of life	XX	XX
Interest rate (i)	X	X
Operating cost factors		
Direct labor	XXX	XX
Indirect labor	XX	XX
Fringe benefits	XX	XX
Maintenance	XX	XX
Power and utilities	XX	XX
Taxes and insurance	X	XX
Total operating cost	XXXX	XXX
Gross saving in operating cost (excludes depreciation and profit tax)		XX
Net saving per year* (gross saving less depreciation and tax)		XX

* Not considering the time value of cash flows.

In evaluating alternative proposals, the more sound approach is to employ present worth concepts and analysis. A simple example will serve to illustrate the engineering economic meaning of present worth. Let us assume we have the opportunity to purchase a machine capable of performing the work formerly done manually at a wage cost of $3,000 per year. Further, assume the life of the capital facility is five years and that our value of money (return on investment) is 10 percent. The question is, "How much can we afford to pay for the machine?" We are asking, "What is the present worth of $3,000 at 10 percent interest for five years?"

The mathematical relation for present worth is:

$$PW = R \left[\frac{(1 + i)^n - 1}{i(1 + i)^n} \right]$$

With the values given in the example we have:

$$PW = 3{,}000 \,(3.7910)$$
$$= \$11{,}373$$

Thus the equivalent alternative to an annual series of disbursements of \$3,000 for five years is paying the total sum of \$11,373 at the beginning of year one. The assumptions are, of course, that the same work is performed and all other charges are negligible. Any machine that can perform the same function for less than \$11,373 represents a saving. At \$10,000, for example, the annual saving is:

$$\text{Saving} = \$3{,}000 - \$10{,}000 \text{ (capital recovery factor)}$$
$$= 3{,}000 - 10{,}000 \,(.2638)$$
$$= \$362$$

The relationships for present worth and the capital recovery factor can be obtained from the *Handbook of Industrial Engineering*, Second Edition (New York: John Wiley & Sons, 1992).

For any project under study, there are many different possibilities in the cash flow in and out of the project. These can be charted and dealt with taking the time value of money into account. Many handheld calculators can perform the detailed calculations required.

NOTES

Chapter 1: Introduction

1. Stephen W. Hawking, *A Brief History of Time* (New York: Bantam, 1988), p. vi.
2. Robert O. Metzger, *Profitable Consulting: Guiding America's Managers into the Next Century* (Reading, Mass.: Addison-Wesley, 1989), p. 50.
3. C. Northcote Parkinson, *The Law of Delay* (Boston: Houghton Mifflin, 1971).
4. United States Department of Labor, Bureau of Labor Statistics, *News*. USDL 91-213.
5. Michael L. Dertouzos, Richard K. Lester, and Robert M. Solow, *Made in America* (Cambridge, Mass.: MIT Press, 1989), pp. 132, 133, 148.
6. Ibid., p. 311.

Chapter 2: Productivity

1. United States Department of Labor, Bureau of Labor Statistics, *Monthly Labor Review*, May 1988.
2. Michael L. Dertouzos, Richard K. Lester, and Robert M. Solow, *Made in America* (Cambridge, Mass.: MIT Press, 1989), p. 31, chart.
3. H. B. Maynard, *Handbook of Business Administration* (New York: McGraw-Hill, 1970), pp. 11-38.
4. Thomas J. Peters and Robert H. Waterman, *In Search of Excellence* (New York: Harper & Row, 1982), p. 10.
5. Mott Souders, *The Engineer's Companion* (New York: John Wiley & Sons, 1966), p. 124.
6. Ibid., p. 105.
7. Robert B. Butler, *Architectural and Engineering Calculations Manual* (New York: McGraw-Hill, 1984), p. 246.

8. T. Baumeister, *Standard Handbook for Mechanical Engineers* (New York: McGraw-Hill, 1958), pp. 6–67.
9. Sharp Electronics Corporation, *Applications for Sharp Scientific Calculator* (Japan: 1983), p. 36.
10. Ibid., p. 38.

Chapter 3: Quality

1. Books on the subject of quality control span the range from presentation of the technical principles to the contextual and managerial aspects. Chronologically, the books range from an early classic by Shewhart (published in 1931) to the more recent publications cited below:

    Robert T. Amsden, Howard E. Butler, and Davida M. Amsden, *SPC Simplified* (White Plains, N.Y.: Quality Resources, 1989). As the back cover states, "This practical book teaches the basics of statistical process control."

    Philip B. Crosby, *Quality without Tears* (New York: New American Library, 1984). An easy-reading "context" book for managers.

    W. Edwards Deming, *Quality, Productivity, and Competitive Position* (Cambridge, Mass.: MIT, Center for Advanced Engineering Study, 1982). Those interested in a comprehensive account of "the Deming management method" are referred to the book by Mary Walton cited later.

    V. R. Dingus and W. A. Golomski, *A Quality Revolution in Manufacturing* (Norcross, Ga.: Industrial Engineering and Management Press, 1988).

    John E. Freund et al., *Modern Elementary Statistics* (Englewood Cliffs, N.J.: Prentice Hall, 1988).

    Eugene L. Grant and Richard S. Leavenworth, *Statistical Quality Control* (New York: McGraw-Hill, 1980).

    Kaoru Ishikawa, *Guide to Quality Control* (White Plains, N.Y.: Quality Resources, 1984).

    J. M. Juran and Frank M. Gryna, *Quality Planning and Analysis* (New York: McGraw-Hill, 1980).

    R. J. Schonberger, *World Class Manufacturing* (New York: Free Press, 1986).

Walter A. Shewhart, *Economic Control of Quality of a Manufactured Product* (New York: Van Nostrand, 1931. Republished in 1980 by the American Society for Quality Control).

Mary Walton, *The Deming Management Method* (New York: Dodd, Mead, 1986). This is an interesting account of Deming's work over the years.
2. James Gleick, *Chaos: Making a New Science* (New York: Viking, 1987), p. 221.
3. Peter Shaffer, *Amadeus*, screen play and original stage play, Michael Hausman and Bertol Ohlsson, executive producers, 1984.

Chapter 4: Material Control Systems

1. Masaaki Imai, *Kaizen: The Key to Japan's Competitive Success* (New York: Random House, 1986).

    Gerald J. Bose and Ashok Rao, "Implementing JIT with MRP II Creates Hybrid Manufacturing Environment," *Industrial Engineering* 20, no. 9 (Sept. 1988), pp. 49–53.

    Johnson A. Edosomwan and Carlena Marsh, "Streamlining the Material Flow Process for Just-in-Time Production," *Industrial Engineering* 21, no. 1 (Jan. 1989), pp. 46–50.

    Wanda Savage-Moore, "The Evolution of a Just-in-Time Environment at Northern Telecom Inc.'s Customer Service Center," *Industrial Engineering* 20, no. 9 (Sept. 1988), pp. 60–63.
2. Robert W. Hall, *Zero Inventories* (Homewood, Ill.: Dow Jones-Irwin, 1983), p. 1. As the author explains, stockless production is a goal to be approached.
3. J. T. Black, *The Design of the Factory with a Future* (New York: McGraw-Hill, 1991), p. 34.
4. Imai, *The Key to Japan's Success*, and Mary Walton, *The Deming Management Method* (New York: Dodd, Mead, 1986), p. 122.
5. Jef Barrett, "IEs at CalComp Are Integrating JIT, TQC and Employee Involvement for 'World Class Manufacturing,'" *Industrial Engineering* 20, no. 9 (Sept. 1988), pp. 26–32.
6. Nicholas P. E. Adams, "A Low-Volume Manufacturing Unit Realizes the Advantages of FMS through Innovative Techniques," *Industrial Engineering* 20, no. 11 (Nov. 1988), pp. 21–27.

    C. Thomas Culbreth and David L. Pollpeter, "A Flexible Manufacturing Cell for Furniture Part Production," *Industrial Engineering* 20, no. 11 (Nov. 1988), pp. 28–34.

Shekhar Nagarkar, "Flexible Manufacturing System Lets Small Manufacturer of Mainframes Compete with Giants," *Industrial Engineering* 20, no. 11 (Nov. 1988), pp. 42–46.
7. ProfitKey International, Inc., Salem, New Hampshire.

Chapter 5: Facilities and Layout

1. The computer programs include: Computerized Relative Allocation of Facilities Technique, Computerized Relationship Layout Planning, Automated Layout Design Program, all from RMA Richard Muther & Associates. Information on these programs is available in H. B. Maynard, *Industrial Engineering Handbook* (New York: McGraw-Hill, 1971), p. 11–56.

Chapter 8: Advance Manufacturing Planning

1. Arthur C. Clarke, *Arthur C. Clarke's July 20, 2019, Life in the 21st Century* (New York: Omni Book, Macmillan, 1986), p. 60.
2. Alvin Toffler's form of future shock is equally applicable to people in companies undergoing rapid change.
3. This expression is reported to have been attributed to a research director of a Dutch firm, but the actual reference has not been located.
4. "A Rose is a rose is a rose," Gertude Stein, "Sacred Emily," 1913, as cited in John Bartlett, ed., *Bartlett's Familiar Quotations* (Boston: Little, Brown, 1991).
5. Comment of Steven Cohen, as reported by correspondent Paul Solman in the "MacNeil/Lehrer News Hour," Sept. 11, 1989.
6. Sanford I. Heisler, *The Wiley Engineer's Desk Reference* (New York: John Wiley & Sons, 1984), p. 392.
7. Gavriel Salvendy, *Handbook of Industrial Engineering* (New York: John Wiley & Sons, 1992, pp. 1320–21.
8. R. E. Scherr, A. H. McHose, Ian P. Campbell, and C. J. Bryan, *Automatic Sewing Method and Apparatus*, Patent no. 3,448,705, June 10, 1969.

Chapter 9: Management, Tools and Technology

1. Lee Sproull and Sara Keisler, "Computers, Networks and Work," *Scientific American*, Sept. 1991, pp. 116, 120, 121, 123.
2. Leon Martel, *Mastering Change* (New York: Mentor, 1986).

3. Marc S. Gerstein, *The Technology Connection: Strategy and Change in the Information Age* (Reading, Mass.: Addison-Wesley, 1987).
4. Peter C. Reid, *Well Made in America* (New York: McGraw-Hill, 1990), p. 13.
5. Robert W. Hall, *Zero Inventories* (Homewood, Ill.: Dow Jones-Irwin, 1983), pp. 308, 309.
6. Donald Petersen, *A Better Idea: Redefining the Way Americans Work* (Boston: Houghton Mifflin, 1991).
7. George Stalk, Jr., and Thomas M. Hout, *Competing against Time: How Time-Based Competition Is Reshaping Global Markets* (New York: Free Press, 1990), p. 5.
8. Keith Lockyer, Alan Muhlemann, and John Oakland, *Production and Operations Management*, 5th ed. (London: Pitman Publishing, 1988), p. 529.
9. Jae K. Shim, Joel G. Seifel, and Abraham J. Simon, *The Vest-Pocket MBA* (Englewood Cliffs, N.J.: Prentice Hall, 1986), pp. 150, 151.
10. *STORM,* STORM Software Inc. Cleveland, Oh.
11. *FlexWork,* MillStone Software, Waltham, Mass.
12. *AutoMod,* AutoSimulations, Inc., Trevose, Pa.
13. *TMS,* Titan Software Corp., Monroeville, Pa.
14. *Malcolm Baldrige National Quality Award,* United States Department of Commerce, National Institute of Standards and Technology, Gaithersburg, Md., 1992.

GLOSSARY

artificial intelligence (AI) Computer system programs that produce results we would normally associate with human intelligence. These expert systems contain a knowledge base, an inference engine, and a user interface. Applications are being developed in many areas of industrial and professional work.

attributes A classification of quality characteristics according to some criteria. Two common classes are good or defective parts.

average The sum of a set of sample values divided by the number of values in the set.

capacity driven systems Programs (software) for material control in which job and order processing is based upon the actual load and capacity of each work center.

capacity planning The determination of the number and kind of machine tools and equipment required to produce a given schedule of parts and/or products.

cellular manufacturing system A system of linked manufacturing work cells in which each cell consists of a group of processes that make a family of parts.

computer integrated manufacturing (CIM) The use of computers in manufacturing, with the integration of function and control in a hierarchy of computer systems.

cost reduction The process and application of reducing the cost of a part, process, or system through improvements in design, materials, methods, or systems.

economic order quantity The determination of the amount of product to be purchased or manufactured on a single order so as to obtain a minimum when evaluating the algebraic sum of ordering cost and carrying cost.

engineering change notice (ECN) A document issued by the engineering department that specifies an engineering design change and the disposition of parts made under an earlier specification.

flexible manufacturing systems (FMS) An integrated system of several programmable machine tools interconnected by work manipulators and controlled by a host computer.

fractal A mathematical object such that when the algorithm is used to represent it visually, it has detailed structure no matter how great the magnification or how closely one looks at it, as in the pattern of a fern.

group technology The selection of (a group of) parts that have similar features and/or operations that can be processed through a group of machines with different functions.

indented bill of materials (B/M) A bill of materials that also reveals the structure and components of each subassembly by indenting the list of components making up that subassembly.

just-in-time (JIT) A material/processing system in which the scheduling of final assembly successively initiates the requirements (work order) for limited quantities of upstream parts and subassemblies in a "pull" system control. In an effective application, one of several values is the reduction of inventory cost.

kanban system (bin/card) An order point scheduling system using fixed lot sizes in the replenishment of stock when the bin/card supply is empty. This is part of the **JIT** system.

line balance A procedure of apportioning the work content of operators or machines so as to obtain equal processing time between operators and/or machines.

machine capability study The determination of the ability of a machine to make parts within the specified dimensions of the part. The analysis compares the spread (6σ) of the output of the machine to the dimensional range specified for the part.

machine scheduling A listing of the order and timing of jobs to be processed on a machine.

management information system (MIS) An information system (usually a computer program) to aid in the performance of management functions.

manufacturing assembly chart A chart showing the form and structure of the components and subassemblies from which a product is constructed.

manufacturing (work) cells A group of machines, generally arranged in a U-shaped process sequence, which processes a family of parts. The process could be operator staffed or employ computer numerical control (CNC).

material requirements planning (MRP) A system employing a master production schedule, the bills of material, lead-time data, inventory, and open order to calculate requirements for materials.

mode The most frequently occurring value (class) in a frequency distribution.

numerical controlled (NC machine) Automatic control of a process performed by a device that makes use of numerical data, usually introduced as the operation is in progress.

operation process (flow) chart A chart showing or listing the sequence of operations of a process.

pattern of individuals A chart showing the consecutive variation in some property of a part, obtained from a repetitive process.

plant layout A plan showing the position and arrangement of the machines, facilities, utilities, services, and aisles in a building shell drawing.

present worth The mathematical relationship (formula) involving compound interest, used to calculate present worths of a stream of cash flows. Also, the system of comparing proposed investments that involves discounting at a known interest rate (representing a cost of capital or a minimum acceptable rate of return) in order to choose the alternative having the highest present value-per-unit of investment.

preventive maintenance (PM) A program that provides for scheduled servicing of machines, facilities, and equipment, aimed at reducing unscheduled down time.

productivity (index) Output per input for one or more factors (e.g., labor or machine hours). The ratio of actual production to standard production.

quality control The operating techniques and activities that are employed to meet quality standards.

reliability The probability that a system will perform a required function under specified conditions for a specified period of time or at a given point in time.

sample distribution A group of items or observations taken randomly from a larger collection of items, which serve to provide information about the population from which the sample was taken.

standard deviation A measure of dispersion of a frequency distribution. It is calculated by summing squared deviations from the mean, dividing the number of items in the group, and taking the square root of the quotient.

standard procedure (standard practice) A description that specifies the procedures to be followed in the execution of some task or function.

statistical control The application of statistical techniques to control quality.

system analysis, design, and synthesis The organized steps in a functional analysis of macro and related subsystems for the purpose of developing and improving the performance of the (whole) system to a set of objectives. The general steps include: definition of the problem and scope of study; statement of objectives and criteria of effectiveness; documentation and functional analysis; development of alternative plans and concepts; and finally, selection, installation, and prove-in of new system or process.

system reliability The probability that a system will be operable, specified as a percent or as a time until breakdown. Also, the ability of a system to perform a required function under stated conditions for a stated period of time.

total quality control (TQC) A concept, when practiced, that involves recognition and participation of the whole organization in achieving the standards of quality.

trouble-shooting chart A diagram or chart listing potential problems, their probable causes, and the solutions.

value engineering (value analysis) Review of components of product costs to evaluate the share of component value, with the object of reducing cost and/or improving performance of the product. The analysis may include design considerations, methods engineering, and similar techniques.

BIBLIOGRAPHY

Ackoff, R. L. *Management in Small Doses.* New York: John Wiley & Sons, 1986.

Adams, Nicholas P. E. "A Low-Volume Manufacturing Unit Realizes the Advantages of FMS through Innovative Techniques." *Industrial Engineering* 20, no. 11 (Nov. 1988), pp. 21–27.

Adams, W. *The Structure of American Industry.* New York: Macmillan, 1990.

Amsden, R. T.; H. E. Butler; and D. M. Amsden. *SPC Simplified.* White Plains, N.Y.: Quality Resources, 1989.

Ansari, A., and B. Modarress. *Just in Time Purchasing.* New York: Free Press, 1990.

Augustine, N. R. *Augustine's Laws.* New York: Viking Penguin, 1986.

Barrett, Jef. "IEs at CalComp Are Integrating JIT, TQC and Employee Involvement for 'World Class Manufacturing.'" *Industrial Engineering* 20, no. 9 (Sept. 1988), pp. 26–32.

Baumeister, T. *Standard Handbook for Mechanical Engineers.* New York: McGraw-Hill, 1958.

Bignell, V.; M. Donner; J. Hughes; C. Pym; and S. Stone. *Manufacturing Systems: Context, Applications and Techniques.* Oxford, Eng.: Basil Blackwell, 1985.

Black, J. T. *The Design of the Factory with a Future.* New York: McGraw-Hill, 1991.

Bose, Gerald J., and Ashok Rao. "Implementing JIT with MRP II Creates Hybrid Manufacturing Environment." *Industrial Engineering* 20, no. 9 (Sept. 1988).

Brandenburg, R. G., and W. K. Fallon. *What Every Manager Needs to Know about Manufacturing.* New York: Amacom, 1983.

Butler, Robert B. *Architectural and Engineering Calculations Manual.* New York: McGraw-Hill, 1984.

Clarke, Arthur C. *Arthur C. Clarke's July 20, 2019, Life in the 21st Century.* New York: Omni Book, Macmillan, 1986.

Clifford, D. K., Jr., and R. E. Cavanagh. *The Winning Performance: How America's High-Growth Midsize Companies Succeed.* New York: Bantam Books, 1985.

Cohen, S. S., and John Zysman. *Manufacturing Matters: The Myth of the Post-Industrial Economy.* New York: Basic Books, 1987.

Cohen, Steven. Comments reported by correspondent Paul Solman in the "MacNeil/Lehrer News Hour," Sept. 11, 1989.

Crosby, Philip B. *Quality without Tears.* New York: New American Library, 1984.

Culbreth, C. Thomas, and David L. Pollpeter. "A Flexible Manufacturing Cell for Furniture Part Production." *Industrial Engineering* 20, no. 11 (Nov. 1988), pp. 28–34.

DeGarmo, E. P.; J. T. Black; and R. A. Kohser. *Materials and Processes in Manufacturing.* New York: Macmillan, 1988.

Deming, W. Edward. *Quality, Productivity, and Competitive Position.* Cambridge, Mass.: MIT, Center for Advanced Engineering Study, 1982.

Dertouzos, Michael L.; Richard K. Lester; and Robert M. Solow. *Made in America.* Cambridge, Mass.: MIT Press, 1989.

Dingus, V., and W. A. Golomski. *A Quality Revolution in Manufacturing.* Norcross, Ga.: Industrial Engineering and Management Press, 1989.

Edosomwan, Johnson A., and Carlena Marsh. "Streamlining the Material Flow Process for Just-in-Time Production." *Industrial Engineering* 21, no. 1 (Jan. 1989).

The Ernst & Young Quality Improvement Consulting Group. *Total Quality: An Executive's Guide for the 1990s.* Homewood, Ill.: Dow Jones-Irwin/APICS, 1990.

Freund, John E., et al. *Modern Elementary Statistics.* Englewood Cliffs, N.J.: Prentice Hall, 1988.

Gerstein, Marc S. *The Technology Connection: Strategy and Change in the Information Age.* Reading, Mass.: Addison-Wesley, 1987.

Gitlow, H. S., and Process Management Institute, Inc. *Planning for Quality Productivity and Competitive Position.* Homewood, Ill.: Richard D. Irwin, 1990.

Gleick, James. *Chaos: Making a New Science.* New York: Viking, 1987.

Grant, Eugene L., and Richard S. Leavenworth. *Statistical Quality Control.* New York: McGraw-Hill, 1980.

Hall, Robert W. *Zero Inventories.* Homewood, Ill.: Dow Jones-Irwin, 1983.

Hawking, Stephen W. *A Brief History of Time.* New York: Bantam, 1988.

Heisler, Sanford I. *The Wiley Engineer's Desk Reference.* New York: John Wiley & Sons, 1984.

Higgins, L. R. *Maintenance Engineering Handbook.* New York: McGraw-Hill, 1988.

Holts, H. *How to Succeed as an Independent Consultant.* New York: John Wiley & Sons, 1983.

Hunt, V. D. *Quality in America: How to Implement a Competitive Quality Program.* Homewood, Ill.: Business One Irwin, 1991.

Hutchins, G. B. *Purchasing Strategies for Total Quality.* Homewood, Ill.: Business One Irwin, 1991.

Imai, M. *Kaizen: The Key to Japan's Competitive Success.* New York: Random House, 1986.

Industrial Engineering Terminology, Revised Edition. Norcross, Ga.: Industrial Engineering and Management Press, 1990.

Ishikawa, Kaoru. *Guide to Quality Control.* White Plains, N.Y.: Quality Resources, 1984.

Juran, J. M. *Juran on Leadership for Quality: An Executive Handbook.* New York: Free Press, 1989.

Juran, J. M., and Frank M. Gryna. *Quality Planning and Analysis.* New York: McGraw-Hill, 1980.

Kindred, A. R. *Data Systems and Management: An Introduction to Systems Analysis and Design.* Englewood Cliffs, N.J.: Prentice Hall, 1985.

Klein, J. *Revitalizing Manufacturing: Text and Cases.* Homewood, Ill.: Richard D. Irwin, 1989.

Kulwiec, R. A. *Materials Handling Handbook.* New York: John Wiley & Sons, 1985.

Lockyer, Keith; Alan Muhlemann; and John Oakland. *Production and Operations Management.* 5th ed. London: Pitman Publishing, 1988.

Martel, Leon. *Mastering Change.* New York: Mentor, 1986.

Mason, R. D., and D. A. Lind. *Statistical Techniques in Business and Economics.* Homewood, Ill.: Richard D. Irwin, 1990.

Maynard, H. B. *Handbook of Business Administration.* New York: McGraw-Hill, 1970.

———. *Industrial Engineering Handbook*. New York: McGraw-Hill, 1971.

Melnyk, S. A., and R. Narasimhan. *Computer Integrated Manufacturing: Guidelines and Applications from Industrial Leaders*. Homewood, Ill.: Business One Irwin, 1991.

Metzger, Robert O. *Profitable Consulting: Guiding America's Managers into the Next Century*. Reading, Mass.: Addison-Wesley, 1989.

Moody, P. E. *Strategic Manufacturing: Dynamic New Directions for the 1990s*. Homewood, Ill.: Dow-Jones Irwin, 1990.

Nagarkar, Shekhar. "Flexible Manufacturing System Lets Small Manufacturer of Mainframes Compete with Giants." *Industrial Engineering* 20, no. 11 (Nov. 1988), pp. 42–46.

National Center for Manufacturing Sciences. *Competing in World-Class Manufacturing: America's 21st Century Challenge*. Homewood, Ill.: Business One Irwin, 1990.

Niebel, B. W.; A. B. Draper; and R. A. Wsysk. *Modern Manufacturing Processing*. New York: McGraw-Hill, 1989.

Noble, D. F. *Forces of Production: A Social History of Industrial Automation*. New York: Oxford University Press, 1984.

Parkinson, C. Northcote. *The Law of Delay*. Boston: Houghton Mifflin, 1971.

Pascale, R. T., and A. G. Athos. *The Art of Japanese Management: Applications for American Executives*. New York: Warner Books, 1981.

Peters, T. *Thriving on Chaos: Handbook for a Management Revolution*. New York: Harper & Row, 1987.

Peters, T. J., and R. H. Waterman. *In Search of Excellence: Lessons from America's Best-Run Companies*. New York: Harper & Row, 1982.

Petersen, Donald. *A Better Idea: Redefining the Way Americans Work*. Boston: Houghton Mifflin, 1991.

Plossl, G. W. *Managing in the New World of Manufacturing: How Companies Can Improve Operations to Compete Globally*. Englewood Cliffs, N.J.: Prentice Hall, 1991.

Potts, M., and P. Behr. *The Leading Edge: CEOs Who Turned Their Companies Around: What They Did and How They Did It*. New York: McGraw-Hill, 1987.

Powers, J. H., Jr. *Computer-Automated Manufacturing*. Westerville, Oh.: Glencoe/McGraw-Hill, 1990.

Reich, R. B. *The Work of Nations: Preparing Ourselves for 21st-Century Capitalism*. New York: Alfred A. Knopf, 1991.

Reid, Peter C. *Well Made in America*. New York: McGraw-Hill, 1990.

Salvendy, Gavriel. *Handbook of Industrial Engineering*. New York: John Wiley & Sons, 1982.

Savage-Moore, Wanda. "The Evolution of a Just-in-Time Environment at Northern Telecom Inc.'s Customer Service Center." *Industrial Engineering* 20, no. 9 (Sept. 1988), pp. 60–63.

Schmitt, N. M., and R. F. Farwell. *Understanding Electronic Control of Automation Systems*. Ft. Worth: Radio Shack, 1983.

Schonberger, R. J. *World Class Manufacturing: The Lessons of Simplicity Applied*. New York: Free Press, 1986.

Shewhart, W. A. *Economic Control of Quality of a Manufactured Product*. New York: Van Nostrand, 1931. Republished in 1980 by the American Society for Quality Control.

Shim, Jae K.; Joel G. Siefel; and Abraham J. Simon. *The Vest-Pocket MBA*. Englewood Cliffs, N.J.: Prentice Hall, 1986.

Smith, B. R. *The Country Consultant*. New York: Plume, 1983.

Souders, Mott. *The Engineer's Companion*. New York: John Wiley & Sons, 1966.

Sproull, Lee, and Sara Kiesler. "Computers, Networks and Work." *Scientific American*. Sept. 1991, pp. 116, 120, 121, 123.

Stalk, George, Jr., and Thomas M. Hout. *Competing against Time: How Time-Based Competition Is Reshaping Global Markets*. New York: Free Press, 1990.

Stark, J. *Handbook of Manufacturing Automation and Integration*. Homewood, Ill.: Business One Irwin, 1989.

Steeples, M. M. *The Corporate Guide to the Malcolm Baldrige National Quality Award: Proven Strategies for Building Quality into Your Organization*. Homewood, Ill.: Business One Irwin, 1991.

Toffler, Alvin. *Future Shock*. New York: Random House, 1970.

Tompkins, J. A. *Winning Manufacturing: The How-To Book of Successful Manufacturing*. Norcross, Ga.: Industrial Engineering and Management Press, 1989.

United States Department of Commerce. *Malcom Baldrige National Quality Award*. Gaithersburg, Md.: National Institute of Standards and Technology, 1992.

United States Department of Labor. Bureau of Labor Statistics. *Monthly Labor Review*.

Vollmann, T. E.; W. L. Berry; and D. C. Whybark. *Manufacturing Planning and Control Systems.* Homewood, Ill.: Business One Irwin, 1991.

Walton, Mary. *The Deming Management Method.* New York: Dodd, Mead, 1986.

Whitten, J. L.; L. F. Bentley; and V. M. Barlow. *System Analysis and Design Methods.* Homewood, Ill.: Richard D. Irwin, 1989.

INDEX

A

ABC inventory system, 5
Adams, Nicholas P. E., 186n
Amsden, Davida M., 185n
Amsden, Robert T., 185n
Arbitrary-edict cost reduction, 113
Artificial intelligence, 4
Assignable causes, 53–54
Attributes, 44–50
Automated Layout Design Program, 187n
Automation
   cycle time and balance worksheet, 142–45
   hardware sewing, 149–50
   present worth analysis, 149
   production rates, 147–48
   schematic diagram, 146
   system reliability, 145–49
Automation planning, 135–51
   inputs, 137–38
   operation flow chart, 140–42
   and personnel, 138
   preliminary considerations, 136
   prove-out concept, 137
   synthesis, 138–49
AUTOMOD program, 163
Average deviation, 50–53

B

Balancing worksheet, 142–45
Barrett, Jef, 186n
Bartlett, John, 187n
Baumeister, T., 185n
Black, J. T., 186n
Bose, Gerald J., 186n
Brief History of Time (Hawking), 4
Bryan, C. J., 187n
Bureau of Labor Statistics, 9, 184n
Butler, Howard E., 185n
Butler, Robert B., 184n

C

Campbell, Ian P., 187n
Capacity-driven systems, 81–82
Capacity planning, 72–73
Capital depreciation rates, 13
Cause/effect diagrams, 158
Clarke, Arthur C., 135, 187n
Cleanpack Company narrative, 38–57
Closed-loop feedback system, 167–68
Cohen, Steven, 138, 187n
Computerized Relationship Layout Planning, 187n
Computerized Relative Allocation of Facilities Technique, 187n
Computer programs and simulations, 161–63
Comsys Company narrative, 110–12
Corporate leadership, 12–13
Cost and standard data, 113
Cost reduction
   by arbitrary edict, 113
   general applications, 121
   personnel qualifications, 114
   planning levels, 13–14
   profit sensitivity analysis, 115
   project execution, 115–22

Cost reduction—*Cont.*
    and project planning, 109
    project selection, 114–15
    project teams, 112–13
    staff and line responsibility, 112
    and value engineering, 109–12
Critical path, 156
Crosby, Philip B., 185n
Culbreth, C. Thomas, 186n
Customers, 164
Cycle time, 142–45

D

Deming, W. Edwards, 167–69, 185n
Dertouzos, Michael L., 184n
Dingus, V. R., 185n

E

Economic analysis, 161, 181–83
Economic order quantity system, 5
Edosomwan, Johnson A., 186n
Employees
    automation planning, 138
    labor-management relations, 13
    and process consultant, 69–70
    training program, 24–26
    well-educated, 13
Engineering economic analysis, 181–83

F

Factory of the future, 135–36
Flexible manufacturing systems, 2, 81
FlexWork software, 162
Freund, John E., 185n
Fujitsu Company, 135
Future shock, 135

G

Gerstein, Marc S., 188n
Gleick, James, 186n

Golomski, W. A., 185n
Government regulation, 13
Grant, Eugene L., 177, 185n
Group technology, 88
Gryna, Frank M., 185n

H

Hall, Robert W., 186n, 188n
Handbook of Industrial Engineering, 183
Hardware sewing automation, 149–50
Hausman, Michael, 186n
Hawking, Stephen W., 4, 184n
Heisler, Sanford I., 187n
Hinge manufacturing, 125–33
Histogram, 158–59
HiTech Machine Company narrative, 13–15
Home Novelty Products Company narrative, 125–33
Hout, Thomas M., 188n

I

Indented bill of materials, 63, 76–80
Industrial analyst, 7
Industrial challenges, 1
Industrial charts, 156–58
Industrial concepts, 4–5
    continuous development, 6–7
    misapplication, 5–6
Internal Revenue Service, 13, 181
Inventory
    indented bill of materials, 76–80
    part-numbering, 69–71
    status report, 73–76
Inventory control systems, 80–82
    and machine scheduling, 68–69
    and product definition, 62–66
    types, 4–5
Inventory pull systems, 154
Ishikawa, Kaoru, 185n

J

JIT; see Just in Time system
July 20, 2019, Life in the 21st Century (Clarke), 135
Juran, J. M., 185n
Just in Time system, 4, 81

K–L

Kanban system, 82
Keisler, Sara, 187n
Labor-management relations, 13
Layout concept, 99
Layout planning, 87–105
Learning curve, 160
Leavenworth, Richard S., 177, 185n
Lester, Richard K., 184n
Line balance, 142
Linked cellular manufacturing system, 82
Lockyer, Keith, 188n

M

Machine capability study, 37–57, 177
  analysis of, 53–57
  average and standard deviations, 50–53
  nature of, 42–43
  variables and attributes, 44–50
Machine cycle time, 142–45
Machine design process, 39–42
Machine development tasks, 56
Machine scheduling, 68–69
Machine tools, 23–24
Machine type grouping, 88
Made in America (Dertouzos, Lester, and Solow), 9
Make-to-order system, 82
Malcolm Baldrige National Quality Award, 163, 174–76, 188n
Management
  chief concerns, 164

Management—*Cont.*
  concepts and graphical tools, 160–63
  development considerations, 153
  progressive, 12–13
Management by objectives, 169
Management charts, 154–59
Manufacturing
  automation planning, 135–51
  changes in technology, 152–54
  cost reduction, 109–22, 121
  machine capability study, 37–57
  as management concern, 164
  material control systems, 59–83
  new product design, 33
  number of plants, 1
  operational audit, 167–76
  plant capacity index, 93–95
  plant facilities and layout, 84–108
  plant organization, 71–72
  product fabrication/assembly sequence, 87–89
  productivity development program, 20
  systems, 2–5
  technical analysis, 123–24
Manufacturing assembly chart, 75, 76–80
Manufacturing cells, 81
Manufacturing context, 92–93
Manufacturing engineering, 2–5, 9–10
  charts, 156–58
  cost reduction, 121
  economic analysis, 181–83
  function, 21, 21
  investing in, 26–35
  potential sources of variation, 55
Manufacturing matrix, 161
Manufacturing planning, 135–36
Marsh, Carlena, 186n
Martel, Leon, 187n
Masaaki, Imai, 186n
Mastering Change (Martel), 152

Material control systems
  capacity planning, 72–73
  changes in, 80–82
  development program, 61–62
  importance, 59
  indented bill of materials, 76–80
  and machine scheduling, 68–69
  manufacturing assembly chart, 75, 76–80
  order-processing system, 66–68
  part-numbering, 69–71
  product definition, 62–66
  Quick-Power Company narrative, 60–80
  status report, 73–76
Materials requirement planning, 4–5, 81–82
Matrix analysis, 161
Maynard, H. B., 184n, 187n
McHose, A. H., 187n
McKinsey 7-S Framework, 26–27
Metzger, Robert O., 184n
MillStone Software, 188n
Moving annual total chart, 154–56
MRP; *see* Materials requirement planning
Muhlemann, Alan, 188n

N

Nagarkar, Shekhar, 187n
National Academy of Engineering, 9–10
Net present value analysis, 161
New product design, 33
Numerical controlling milling machine, 34

O

Oakland, John, 188n
Ohlsson, Bertil, 186n
Operating systems, 21–22
Operation flowchart, 140–42
Order-processing system, 66–68

P

Pareto chart, 156
Parkinson, C. Northcote, 9, 184n
Part-numbering, 69–71
Payback period method, 181–82
P chart, 158–59
Performance appraisals, 167–69
Peters, Thomas J., 26, 184n
Peterson, Donald, 188n
Planning levels, 113–14
Plant capacity index, 93–95
Plant consolidation/integration, 91–97
Plant facilities and layout, 84–108
  economic factors, 95–97
  general approach, 97–105
  plan components, 89
  travel chart, 160–61
  types, 87–105
Plant organization, 71–72
Pollpeter, David L., 186n
Present worth analysis, 149
Problem/solution chart, 157–58
Process consultant, 6–7
  and employee anxiety, 69–70
  technical analysis, 123–24
Process control, 35–57
Product
  definition, 62–66
  management concern, 164
  variables and attributes, 44–50
Product design, cost reduction, 121
Product fabrication/assembly sequence, 87–89
Production
  capacity planning, 72–73
  cost reduction, 109–22
  factory of the future, 135–36
  indented bill of materials, 76–80
  inventory control systems, 80–82
  learning curve, 160
  machine scheduling, 68–69
  manufacturing assembly chart, 75, 76–80
  manufacturing context, 92–93

Production—*Cont.*
  plant facilities and layout, 84–108
  quality control chart, 177–79
  rapid changes in levels of, 65–66
  status report, 73–76
  technical analysis, 123–24
  work flow, 91–92
Production control department, 79
Production rate, 147–48
Productivity
  definition and rates, 11–12
  development program, 20
  engine of economic vitality, 9
  factors affecting, 12–35
  importance, 11
  improving, 15–20
  investing in manufacturing engineering, 26–35
  long-range, 124
  machine tools, 23–24
  manufacturing engineering function, 21
  process control study, 35–37
  quality control program, 24
  upgrading operating systems, 21–22
  work flow, 22–23
Productivity centers, 11
Product life cycles, 160
Product structure tree, 63, 76
ProfitKey International, Inc., 187n
ProfitKey software, 81–82
Profit sensitivity analysis, 115
Program evaluation and review technique (PERT) chart, 156
Progressive management, 12–13
Project execution, 115–22
Project schedule chart, 156
Project selection, 114–15
Project teams, 112–13
Prove-out concept, 137

Q

Quality control
  principles, 37
  program, 24

Quality control chart, 177–79
  types, 158–59
Quick-Power Company narrative, 60–80

R

Rao, Ashok, 186n
Reid, Peter C., 188n
Results-oriented analysis, 169
RMA Richard Muther & Associates, 187n

S

Sales forecast, 72
Salvendy, Gavriel, 187n
Savage-Moore, Wanda, 186n
Scatter diagram, 156
Scherr, R. E., 187n
Schonberger, R. J., 185n
Seifel, Joel G., 188n
Shaffer, Peter, 186n
Sharp Electronics Corporation, 185n
Shewart, Walter A., 186n
Shim, Jae K., 188n
Simon, Abraham J., 188n
Single-location assembly, 88
Solman, Paul, 187n
Solow, Robert M., 184n
Souders, Mott, 184n
Southern/Bell Furniture Company narrative, 85–105
Sproull, Lee, 187n
Staff and line responsibility for cost reduction, 112
Stalk, George, Jr., 188n
Standard deviation, 50–53
Standard procedure instruction, 79
Statistical control, 41
  assignable causes, 53–54
  average and standard deviations, 50–53
Statistical Quality Control (Grant and Leavenworth), 177

Status report, 73–76
Stein, Gertrude, 138, 187n
Stockless production; *see* Just in Time system
STORM program, 162
STORM Software Inc., 188n
Structural analysis, 169
System analysis, 167
　design, and synthesis, 8–9
System reliability, 145–49
　present worth analysis, 149
　production rate, 147–48

T

Technical analysis
　hinge manufacturing, 125–33
　problems, 123–24
Technology
　automation, 135–51
　changes in, 152–54
Technology Connection (Gerstein), 152
Time value of cash flows, 181–82
Titan Software Corporation, 188n
Toffler, Alvin, 187n

Total Maintenance System program, 163
Total quality control, 5
Total quality control program, 81
Training program, 24–26
Transient response system, 167
Travel chart, 160–61

U–V

Unions, 13
United States Department of Labor, 184n
Value added concept, 106
Value engineering, 109–12
Variables, 44–50
Variance chart, 156

W–X

Walton, Mary, 185n, 186n
Waterman, Robert H., 26, 184n
Work-cell manufacturing layout, 88
Work flow, 91–92
　line balance, 142
　and productivity, 22–23
X, R charts, 158–59